Letters from Florence

Also from Marie-Laure Valandro and Lindisfarne Books:

Camino Walk: Where Inner & Outer Paths Meet

Observations on the Inner Art of Travel

MARIE-LAURE VALANDRO

Lindisfarne Books

2010
Lindisfarne Books
an imprint of Anthroposophic Press/SteinerBooks
Main St., Great Barrington, MA
www.steinerbooks.org

Copyright © 2010 by Marie-Laure Valandro. All rights reserved.
No part of this publication may be reproduced, stored in a retrieval system, or transmitted, in any form or by any means, electronic, mechanical, photocopying, recording, or otherwise, without the prior written permission of the publisher.

Cover & book design: William Jens Jensen
All photographs copyright © by Marie-Laure Valandro

LIBRARY OF CONGRESS CATALOGING-IN-PUBLICATION DATA

Valandro, Marie-Laure.
 Letters from Florence : observations on the inner art of travel / Marie-Laure Valandro.
     p. cm.
 ISBN-13: 978-1-58420-082-6
 ISBN-10: 1-58420-082-0
 1. Florence (Italy)—Description and travel. 2. Valandro, Marie-Laure—Travel—Italy—Florence. 3. Spiritual biography. 4. Florence (Italy)—Social life and customs. 5. Florence (Italy)—Religious life and customs. 6. Church buildings—Italy—Florence. 7. Florence (Italy)—Buildings, structures, etc. I. Title.
 DG734.23.V35 2010
 945'.511—dc22
                                                          2010012925

To my mother Paulette Valandro; to my sisters Beatrice, Elizabeth, and Veronica; to my daughter Ladan; and to my friends Dorothea, Yanny, Bente, Kate, Fiorenza, Mary, Angela, Sonya, Ruth S., Ruth Z., Ruth D., Sandy, Mary, Jody, Aisha, Goldpar, Celia, Martina, Adrian, Helen, Chantal, Carmen, Roberta, Betsy, Gertrude, Joyce, Susan, Anne R., Loti, J.D., Gail, Michele, and many others.

Foreword

"Those who write books suitable for meditative content have a great temptation to overcome. There are books about the highest truths that, when we read them, seem to send a frosty breeze and a certain reserve and dryness in the reader. And there are other books that send the reader emotional warmth and overflowing glow. This latter kind is enchanting for many people, and consequently many prefer it to the former. Therein lays the temptation for authors to write their own feelings and enthusiasm into the message to convey such emotions to the reader. What effect does this have on readers? When writers manage to hold back their own feelings—offering only pure, chaste, truthful thoughts as a temple, like pure, chaste mystery temples of the ancient world—through pure thoughts alone something will light up in pupils, leading them to and kindling in them the heights of knowledge. However, writings that are flooded with the writer's emotions affect the reader as a consuming fire that does not allow the reader's own sparks to rise." —Rudolf Steiner[1]

The text you are about to read has such elements, though the temptation was certainly not always overcome. However, when you come to passages that are a bit hard and dry, you will know the reasons.

To exist in our time, Anthroposophy must use the means provided by today's civilization. In books and lectures, it must find its way to human beings, but it is not in nature of the "library shelf." It must be born anew in the human heart each time one turns to a written book to learn of it. This cannot happen unless the author has looked into human hearts

---
1 Rudolf Steiner, October 29, 1909 (private publication).

while writing in order to discover what must be said to them. People cannot do this unless they are touched by the living Spirit as they write. Then they will confide to the dead written word something that the soul of the reader, who is seeking the Spirit, can experience as a resurrection of the word's Spirit form. Only books that can come to life in human beings as they read may be called anthroposophic.[2]

In their hearts, people should make a gift to the gods of all the truths acquired as images of the outer world. People should always say to themselves: When I obtain knowledge, I remove it from the progressive stream. Be clear that the acquisition of knowledge must be in the service of the gods. There is another kind of knowledge, untouched by any awareness of the holy service that knowledge gives to developing humanity. Such knowledge is taken away from the outer world but not given to the gods, who would be nourished by what they would thus receive. Knowledge not gathered in this spirit but taken without gratitude is like grains of wheat that fall to the earth and rot. In other words, it serves no real goal—neither its own nor that of becoming nourishment for human beings.... Today, humankind has not yet developed much of a feeling for knowledge as divine service....

In the ancient mysteries and mystery schools, it was simply assumed that those who acquired knowledge would treat it with holy regard. Indeed, this was one of the main reasons for not admitting everyone. Those who were admitted had to guarantee that they would regard the knowledge as holy and treat it as service to the gods.... Today, it is necessary for people to achieve this attitude once more.[3]

A properly written anthroposophic book should *awaken* the spiritual life of the reader, and not merely be a collection of information. Reading it should be more than reading; it should be an experience accompanied by inner shocks, tensions, and resolutions.[4]

We must make our life into a school for learning. Life is a school for learning for the fewest number of people. Most people surrender themselves to pleasure and pain. When life passes over them, pain, joy, and comfort pass over. They learn nothing at all from their lives. On the

---

[2] Rudolf Steiner, January 24, 1924 (private publication).

[3] Rudolf Steiner, *The Riddle of Humanity: The Spiritual Background of Human History* (London: Rudolf Steiner Press, 1990), pp. 77–78 (translation revised).

[4] Rudolf Steiner, *Autobiography: Chapters in the Course of My Life, 1861–1907* (Great Barrington, MA: SteinerBooks, 2006), p. 224.

other hand, an anthroposophist says that everyday must take one forward; every day must be a step of one's development.[5]

There are four spheres of human activities in which we can dedicate ourselves to the Spirit by killing all selfish life. These are the spheres of knowledge, art, religion, and the loving, spiritual dedication to a person. Whoever does not live in at least one of these four spheres does not live at all. Knowledge is dedication to the universal in thoughts; art is dedication to the universal in contemplation; religion is dedication to the universal feeling; and love is dedication—with all our spiritual forces—to something that seems to us to be an invaluable being in the world totality. Knowledge is the most spiritual form of selfless dedication, and love is the most beautiful. Love is the true light of heaven in everyday life. Love ennobles our being right into our innermost fiber. It lifts all that lives in us. Pure, devout love transforms our whole soul life into another life that has a relationship with the world Spirit. In this highest sense, to love means to bear the breadth of divine life where mostly shameful egotism and careless passion are to be found. Before we may speak of devotion, we must know something of the holiness of love.

Those who have passed out of separateness and lived through one of these four spheres and into divine life have reached the goal for which the seed of yearning was placed in their hearts—union with the Spirit. This is a true definition. Those who live in the spirit, live free; they have freed themselves form all secondary things. Nothing compels them, other than that by which they are gladly compelled, for they have known it as the highest.

Let truth come to life. Lose yourself in order to find yourself again in the world of spirit.[6]

---

5 Rudolf Steiner, Berlin Feb. 13, 1904 (private publication).

6 Rudolf Steiner, *Start Now! A Book of Soul and Spiritual Exercises* (Great Barrington, MA: SteinerBooks, 2004), pp. 46–47.

A neighborhood in Florence

Letters from Florence

It has taken two hours to figure out this bloody laptop. Now I can start typing, but I have forgotten what I was going to say. In any case, I am in my Florence abode following a hellish entrance to this city. Where are the bloody Italians? It has everything but Italians—every nationality, including lots of Spaniards. Where I am, behind the train station, Florence looks much like a third-world country. Although the streets are cleaned each night, it looks dirty, perhaps because I just arrived from Munich, which is incredibly clean. The tall glasses of German beer are replaced by small cups of coffee, with pizza and pizza and pizza. My room is not the palace one pictures when thinking of Florence, but the narrowest of rooms, barely wide enough that I don't hit the walls on either side. A whole family lives in the tiny kitchen with a computer and a TV on. The kitchen table and related things are all in the narrow corridors. I am staying on the top floor, great for lugging all my stuff—forty pounds of books, a laptop, clothes, and my pocketbook. I carried all that stuff around Florence after leaving the train station about 11 p.m.

It was pouring rain, but I was too cheap to take a taxi. I ended up taking a bus, but I had no ticket because I had been unable to figure out how to get one before boarding. I was headed to a place for backpackers, which I'd discovered through a leaflet in a Munich youth hostel. It seems I continue to travel the way I did thirty years ago, not yet realizing that I am no longer a "youth." But it didn't matter; the hostel has disappeared.

So I found myself on the cobblestone streets with my eighty pounds of bags. It was still pouring outside, and the cobblestones were not a great match for the little wheels of my suitcases. It was almost midnight and everyone was heading home as I swore every name in the book in English and French. I finally entered a hotel, where I asked someone to call a taxi for me, which took me to another hotel so full no one would even respond to me.

One poor soul must have heard me swearing before he opened the door to let me in. I climbed the stairs with my things to the sixth floor and was exhausted as I returned to the lobby. I left everything at the hotel and, after grabbing a magazine to keep the main entry from locking, I left to find a place to stay. After about an hour, I found another building and approached a Somalian man, who told me he had a room similar to the one I had gotten. By the early morning hours, I was tucked safely into my skinny bed in my skinny room with my extra skinny towels—probably dish towels—and no soap. All of this for fifty dollars U.S. . . a real bargain. It felt as though I was in an African country.

My laptop is not very happy about my careless use of grammar and syntax. It keeps saying don't do this, don't do that, bad writing, and so on. Get creative, will you? During the night I kept hearing a strange sound on the cobblestones—tourists passing with rolling suitcases, looking for a place to stay or in the process of leaving. I have never seen anything like this, and I have traveled quite a bit. It seems everyone had been thinking, *Lets go to Florence,* but the Italians must have exodussed (yes, computer, I made up a word). When I asked a waitress where all the Italians had gone, she said they were busy taking care of the millions of tourists who come here.

I must have walked at least a dozen miles, from the train station through the famous great piazzas and over bridges, looking for a place to rent for a month. I went to a piazza near the Piazza Santa Croce to meet a woman who had advertised an apartment to share. Along the way, I passed an Islamic center, where men were hanging around as they would back home in their original countries. It felt as though I were near the bazaar in Tehran.

I found the entrance to the woman's place a few doors down the square, and she opened it to me. She was very sweet, probably my age and tiny. She showed me up the stairs and into a cavernous, dark apartment; bombs could not destroy it. Great cement pillars as only the Italians can build them. It was untidy and a bit dirty. The woman said that in fact she did not have anything at the moment, because the upstairs was being renovated and, of course, I could not sleep in the middle of that mess. But she said that she had a house on the sea in some town and that I could stay there until the apartment was done. From the looks of it, I thought it would take a few more days than she expected. The woman even gave me a train ticket to go there, and she would have a taxi fetch me to the house from the train station. I almost took her up on it, but decided that I needed a rest after the past couple of days. I returned to my narrow residence near the train station and got a room on the next floor—of course, my room had been rented. What a fiasco! I recalled the time I was in Florence thirty years earlier. I had been driving a Peugeot purchased in France all the way to Tehran. Except for the *Duomo,* much of Florence escaped my notice at the time.

As I walk all day around this city, it seems that it must have been exactly the same at the time of Dante, the streets filled with Africans, Arabs, Romani, French, Germans, Japanese, Chinese, and just about every other nationality in the world. The streets are so full of the world, it must be quite different for those who live here. Imagine that you cannot have your country to yourself. It's worse than Paris in that way. Far worse. We must be grateful to the Italians for being so gracious to us foreigners. If I were Italian, I think I'd be swearing at the tourists all day. A friend of my daughter told me that the locals stay out of town until winter, after most of the tourists have gone home. That's when they get their city back.

In Dante's *Divine Comedy* ("Paradise"), his great-great-grandfather describes the Florence of his day:

> father of your grandfather, was my son.
>   And meet it were that you offer your prayers
>   to shorten the long sentence of his weight
>
> Florence, enclosed within her ancient walls
>   from which she still hears terce and nones rings out,[1]
>   once lived in peace, a pure and temperate town:
>
> no necklace or tiara did she wear,
>   no lavish gowns or fancy belts that were
>   more striking than the woman they adorned,
>
> In those days fathers had no cause to fear
>   a daughter's birth: the marriageable age
>   was not too low, the dowry not too high.

---

1 *Terce* is at 9:00 a.m., *nones* at 3:00 p.m.

> Houses too large to live in were not built,
>   and Sardanapalus had not yet come
>   to show to what use bedrooms can be put.
>
> Not yet had your Uccellatoi surpassed
>   Rome's Montemalo, which in its ascent
>   being surpassed, will be so in its fall.
>
> Bellincion Berti I have seen walk by
>   belted in leather and bone, and his good wife
>   come from her mirror with unpainted face;
>
> de'Nerli I have seen, del Vecchio too,
>   content to wear plain leather, and their wives
>   to handle flax and spindle all day long.
>
> O happy wives! Each one of them was sure
>   of her last resting place—none of them yet
>   lay lonely in her bed because of France.
>
> One watching tenderly above the cradle,
>   soothing her infant in that idiom
>   which all new parents love to use at first;
>
> another, working at her spinning-wheel
>   surrounded by her children, would tell tales
>   about the Trojans, Rome, and Fiesole....
>
> To this serene, this lovely state of being
>   within this comity of citizens,
>   joined in good faith, this dwelling-place so sweet.[2]

And why am I here? Well it has to do with my daughter Ladan, who decided to live in Barcelona, alone, at nineteen (almost twenty), because the university in the Midwest is too boring, and she wants to work and be on her own etc. So she teaches English while learning Spanish, and of course she can visit her new Italian friend who lives in Fiesole, a town about five miles northeast of Florence. My husband and I thought that I should at least be within reach, and since I was going to be in Europe for a conference, I would extend my

---

[2] Dante, *The Divine Comedy, Volume 3: Paradise*, lines 94–126, translated by Mark Musa (New York: Penguin, 1986), pp. 181–182.

stay a bit. I would be a short flight away from Barcelona in case she needs her *mom*. Okay, its more like we need to reassure ourselves.

Florence is not Barcelona, so it is not as obvious that I am being nosy. I am a painter in an artistic city, and I told my daughter that I am here to study, to finish writing something, and that between writing and seeing museums, churches, and drinking cappuccinos, I might be available just in case. But I don't think anyone can fool a twenty-year-old these days. If not for my daughter, I would be at home on the farm and not looking at the Madonnas of Florence. (I do not even paint Madonnas; I prefer painting the Grail king.) Things kind of develop on their own.

Three months ago, I had no idea I would be in Florence, just as my daughter had any idea she would be in Spain. It seems to run in the family. At home we believe in the unexpected. All this to say why I started writing undated letters between my other writings. So let us get on.

A few days later...more churches and museums. This city is bottomless in its cultural riches. I have gotten lost every day in this city, and in the past four days I have not revisited any of the same streets. There are so many new churches and museums. I already have a favorite, off the Piazza della Repubblica, where there is an extraordinary painting of the virgin and child. Every time I pass by the small chapel, I have to stop to admire it. It is forbidden to take pictures, but I have disobeyed (like all good Italians) and took a picture, though not a good one. In any case, I have another month to sneak back in. Last night there was a concert featuring a few pieces of organ music and harpsichord. While listening to the pieces, I stared at the picture the whole time. The picture must have been painted around the 1450s. It has no perspective and was made when artists still gilded their works with gold. Everyone seemed captivated by the magic of the painting, there almost alone and dominating the space—much better than all those cathedrals that contain endless paintings to view and where one's eyes become lost in all the richness. In this simple chapel, one can actually feel the power of that painting.

So I meditated on what actually created such power. The subject, of course, but the painter himself must have had a real experience of the Mother and child or the eternal Sophia. Her cloak is a deep blue, almost black, because of the light and great vermilion red for her dress.

This city is one big hotel, one big restaurant, one big church, and one big museum. There are thousands of restaurants in Florence; it's a big job to feed all of the people who come day after day to see the magnificent, indescribable palaces, churches, and other sights. People from everywhere come here to bathe in the city's history and culture. It is actually too much to take in such a wealth of impressions, and one finds it difficult to digest its renaissance culture and history. It seems they had no limit; they just decided to keep building more and more palaces, churches, and cathedrals. Painters, sculptors, writers, architects, poets, dramatists, theologians, musicians, dressmakers, as well as all the artisan guilds. What do we build today that can replace such powerfully meaningful manifestations of their activities? Not much, I must admit, except for going to the Moon and Mars and making ever-more cars and clothes, making more wars, and finding more oil, gold, and silver while polluting the Earth.

The gods are gone or are leaving us alone, and we no longer find much meaning in painting such magnificent works of Christian art. The rules are gone, and we are left on our own to find the answers (or not). Nowadays, we mostly find no answers, so we fill the empty space with more material and endemic shopping sprees that leave the soul forever wanting more.

I slept in another BED and then breakfast. Everyone here seems to have made their homes into B and *no* B's. Noisy streets, the familiar rolling suitcases as tourists arrive and depart after their orgies of culture to return home, where they are not surrounded by nice cathedrals. It's not fair that Florence should distribute such fabulous riches—there is far too much to appreciate. On Wednesday I have an appointment at the Uffizi Gallery to see yet more paintings. Thousands of them are waiting for me.

Thanks to the mother of my daughter's friend, I obtained a room in a very nice large old villa outside of Florence. It has lots of land, an olive orchard, with my favorite, fig trees, intermingled among the olive trees. I used to eat figs from a fig tree when I was six years old and lived in Morocco. In our garden we had two huge fig trees, one red and one golden. For supper that first night, I stepped into the garden and had a few delightful figs, I felt like I was a child again.

The house if full of men. The owner says he has two sons and three brothers, and the cleaning person is a man as well, from the Far East. Except a few older aunts, it seems the women have gone. The beautiful gardens seem idyllic to me, and it's great place to stay.

The world is getting stranger and marriages are no longer seen as sacred. Women are left on their own after raising children and losing their youthful freshness. Men remarry and so it goes, on and on. What are we to do with all these older women who are set aside. The children are raised and gone on their own, the husbands are free. What a world. Can we find new ways for women and men to live together? Perhaps big houses for friends, and friends of friends, to share some time together. Marriage certainly doesn't seem to work anymore, since one out of two ends in divorce.

I read somewhere that in the old days, husband and wives did not spend so much time together. A couple might be together for perhaps three months out of a whole year; the men worked, went to war, traveled for business, and so on. Maybe that's the answer.

It seems as though I've been wandering the streets of Florence for days. Yesterday, I had to do some vegetable shopping, and of course it took me all morning to do a few errands by bus. I have to get more organized. The fruits from the market are great, as well as the various cheeses. Since I have my own farm and garden, I love to chat with the growers. Their faces are hardy, formed by the seasons and harsh wind. They resemble the land that takes care of them.

Why can't we in the U.S. have the Venetians' love of preparing food? Everything becomes an art here, a quality I hope they never lose. In North

America, we must return to quality of food instead of quantity, which is leading to serious problems.

In his *La Bella Figura: Field Guide to the Italian Mind,* one of my favorite contemporary Italian writers, Beppe Severgnini, says:

> Let's see now : unaffectedness; self-indulgence; habit; relief; confidence; imagination; recollections; curiosity; lashings of intuition; a pinch of tradition; family, civic, and regional pride; diffidence; conformism; intransigence; realism; ostentation; amusement; and surprising serenity. These are the emotions Italians experience as they prepare to sit at a restaurant table. You should try to experience them, instead of just ordering linguini primavera.
>
> In short, we are consummate professionals of culinary consumption. No one else in Europe eats the way we do. The French know what they are talking about, but they're sliding into affectation. They tend to be fussy, and overdo the sauces. France offers late-Empire cooking, as charming as end-of-summer roses. Italy still has republican vigor grafted onto tradition. For centuries, Italians have sought and usually found, consolation at the table. We don't think that a sauce is tasty, or that olive oil is good. We know it is....
>
> Note that I am talking about all Italians, not just a hard core of gastronomes. There is a spontaneous gustatory proficiency that cuts across social classes, age groups, income brackets, education, and geographical boundaries....
>
> Of course, Italy, too, is changing, and picking up bad habits.... We eat too much, too often. A century ago, children were toothpick-thin. Seventy years ago, they were slim; forty years ago, they looked well nourished. Today they are overweight. We are increasingly tolerant of precooked and frozen meals. We still have not descended to American TV dinners, the graveyard of family conversation, but the TV set is on, and the microwave is waiting....
>
> If we want to save the Italian way of eating, we have to focus on pride and distrust, qualities we have in abundance.[3]

I went to various churches again yesterday, but the opulence is a bit stifling; there is nowhere for the eyes to rest. It is the price we pay for living in modern times. Many of the old masterpieces belonging to the churches are

---

3 Beppe Severgnini, *La Bella Figura: A Field Guide to the Italian Mind* (Broadway Books, 2006), p. 21–23.

now in museums, leaving the churches with empty spaces. Often those empty spaces have been filled with other works of art that do not belong. This mix-and-match method disturbs those spaces and creates a salad of styles. The original icon paintings that are so valuable have been replaced by larger paintings of later centuries that lack the effect of the original icons.

Nonetheless, this is just the way it looks now, though originally it must have been more unified. The churches, or cathedrals, are quite rectangular, with domes placed variously around the rectangle. While the Italians were very busy with paintings, the French were busy designing cathedrals to assault the heavens, through both the stonework and the work of the mind (Aquinas). The "sacred spaces" of French cathedrals do not really need the added opulence of paintings; just glorious stained glass. There, the walls and intricate arches speak, with no need of massive dome paintings. But here, the walls bear marvelous storybooks, and being a painter myself, I love them all. One must remember that in the old days, most people could not read and lived more in the imaginative realm, learning through paintings and murals. Their hearts were not as closed off as ours are today. These sacred works of art touched them very deeply and formed their souls—or seen from another perspective, what lived in their hearts and in their artist's hearts shaped the masterpieces.

Beppe Severgnini points out about his fellow Italians and art:

> There's an expression in Italian that sums up this attitude, *roba da museo* (museum fodder). The painter and writer Emilio Tadini said that a painting, an object, a program, an idea, or a proposal could be museum fodder. It had to be "something outside life, buried in the past, that has absolutely nothing to do with us." Why? Perhaps it's a feeling of discomfort. Our forebears were so brilliant we prefer to avoid comparisons. Or perhaps, as I was saying, we are too used to museum fodder. We simmer perennially in beauty, and feel we shouldn't have to buy a ticket to go and see some.
>
> In Italy's parish recreation grounds, ancient frescoes gaze down on the children playing soccer. For us, this is normal.... Italy has most of the planet's artistic heritage. Spain comes after us, but has less than you can find in Tuscany alone. But, with a few exceptions, even this no longer excites us. Unless we can make some cash out of it, or impress the rest of the world.[4]

---

4 Ibid., p. 72.

La Galleria degli Uffizi

This morning I had to get up early, I made my appointment for the Uffizi gallery at 8:30, and I got there just on time, as there was already an enormous line, everyone chatting and coming from all corners of the world. They were different ages, backgrounds, social levels. What diplomacy does not do, *art* does. Instead of training diplomats, we should send artists to be diplomats; they speak a common language. It would not be a question of peace and war, but of making art.

We got into the museum twenty minutes later. My favorite paintings are from early 1200 to 1400. One really cannot compare them to anything else. Though I really enjoy the early works, it is difficult to explain why. I am not a historian or expert, but as a painter I will try. Those early paintings seem to draw your attention more and hold it. Perhaps it is the gold with the lapis lazuli and great vermilion-cinnabar that give those works a kind of magic. The words of Dante from *Paradise* canto XIII seem to fit. He paints with words the way those artists painted with colors:

>All that which dies and all that cannot die
>>reflect the radiance of that Idea
>>which God the Father through His love begets:
>
>that Living Light, which from its radiant Source
>>streams forth its light but never parts from it
>>nor from the Love which tri-unites with them,
>
>of its own grace sends down its rays, as if
>>reflected, through the nine subsistencies,
>>remaining sempiternally Itself.
>
>Then it descends to the last potencies,
>>from act to act becoming so diminished,
>>it brings forth only brief contingencies;
>
>and by this term I mean things generated,
>>things which the moving heavens produce from seed
>>or not from seed. The wax of things like these
>
>is more or less receptive, and the power
>>that shapes it, more or less effective—stamped
>>with the idea, it shines accordingly.

> So trees of the same species may produce
> dissimilar fruit, some better and some worse;
> so men are born with diverse natural gifts.
>
> And if the wax were perfectly disposed,
> and if the heavens were at their highest power,
> the brilliance of the seal would shine forth full;
>
> but Nature never can transmit this light
> in its full force—much like the artisan
> who knows his craft but has a trembling hand.
>
> But if the Fervent Love moves the Clear Vision
> of the First Power and makes of that its seal,
> the things it stamps is perfect in all ways.
>
> And this is how the dust of earth was once
> made fit to form the perfect living being
> and how the Virgin came to be with child.
>
> And so you see how right you are to think
> that human nature never has been since
> nor ever will be such, as in those two.[5]

One cannot express it better, and the painters cannot reproduce better than what I am seeing now. Rudolf Steiner said this about Mary:

> Throughout the middle ages there was a sublime preparation for spiritually engendering the opposite sex in people. Human beings developed in themselves by concentrating—at first as a thought—what had to become a reality in them later on. Therefore, as a preparation for this, during the Middle Ages the cult of Mary resulted. This is nothing other than concentrating to engender the female in the male, while for the female the cult of Jesus served the parallel purpose. The cult of Mary had its origin in this foundation.[6]

Now back to the sacred paintings. The painters of those days could still feel the ancient power of the sacred word; they had not completely separated into subject versus the object; they were still one with the observed—the opposite of seventeenth-century Cartesian dualism. Hence, when they painted the Madonna and child, they lived it. We still benefit from their subtle loving

---

5 Dante, *The Divine Comedy, Volume 3: Paradise*, lines 52–87, pp. 160–161.
6 Rudolf Steiner, *The Temple Legend: Freemasonry and Related Occult Movements* (London: Rudolf Steiner Press, 2002), p. 224–225.

Madonna and Child detail, Adoration Of The Magi *(1488),*
by Domenico Ghirlandaio, Galleria dell'Ospedale degli Innocenti, Florence

souls and the spirit that guided their hands. In some one can truly say that the angels are painting, the faces are exquisite.

We see a transition from pyramids and temples to Romanesque churches—monuments again of inner creative power. We see how, from the sixth century AD onward, the cross bearing the dead Jesus makes its appearance in art. And gradually out of the stream of Christianity, a remarkable figure appears, one whose mysteries are very deeply hidden. We may picture this figure in the wonderful form given to it through the painter's art in Raphael's *Sistine Madonna*. This virginal woman at the center of the picture with the child in her arms is well known. Certainly those who have seen it experienced a sensation of awe. It is a wonderful expression of the spiritual striving of humanity. One thing to notice about this picture is that it was not without purpose that Raphael surrounded his Madonna with clouds, from which many angelic forms, like little children, appear.

Let us allow our feelings to be completely taken up with this picture—feelings deep enough that one can sense something very different from what ordinary understanding might grasp. Do not these cloud-like angels around the Madonna have a special meaning? They convey something of the greatest significance if we contemplate them deeply enough. As we are absorbed in this picture, something murmurs in our soul, suggesting that here is a miracle in the best sense of the word; surely this child in the arms of the madonna was not given birth by woman in an ordinary way. These wonderfully delicate forms of angels in the clouds seem to be in process of coming into being, while the child in the Madonna's arms seems to be a denser manifestation of them, like something that has crystallized more strongly than these fleeting angelic forms. Brought down from the clouds and held fast in her arms—that is how the child appears to us, not as if born from the woman; it alludes to a mysterious connection between the child and virgin mother. If we evoke this picture before our souls, another virgin mother appears—the Egyptian Isis with the child Horus. We may sense a mysterious connection between the Christian Madonna and the Egyptian figure known to us as Isis, on whose temple were inscribed the words "I am what was, and what is, and what will be; my veil no mortal can pierce."

The miracle we have hinted at in the picture of the Madonna is also indicated in Egyptian myth. Horus was not fathered by ordinary conception, but a beam of light is said to have fallen from Osiris upon Isis. A kind of immaculate birth took place and the child Horus appeared.

Thus we see how various threads are interwoven, though without an earthly connection....

Isis was connected in a mysterious way with the whole art of healing. In this respect, she was regarded as the teacher of the Egyptian priesthood. In the final stages of antiquity, it was said that Isis, even while among the immortals, still took a special interest in the art of healing, in the health of humankind. All this implies very mysterious connections....

By uplifting the self to what was spiritual, in ancient times there was a healing element, and it would be well if people came to understand this again.... [Looking to] the future, people will not be subjected to the somnambulistic sleep [the initiation of Egyptian temple sleep]. Self-consciousness will be fully maintained, but a strong spiritual power will become active in human beings, and then having wisdom and insight into higher worlds will again be able to bring harmony and healing to human nature. This connection between spirituality and healing is so hidden today that those who are not initiated to some degree into the deeper wisdom of the mysteries know little of it. They cannot perceive the subtle processes involved. However, those with more penetrating insights know deep, inner conditions upon which healing may depend....

The priests of ancient Egypt knew this, and they knew that the farther they guided human vision back into earlier conditions, the nearer they would bring them into conditions of existence with no illness. Even a mere vision of the old Atlantean gods could have a curative effect, but this was even stronger when the priests guided these visions in such a way that the "temple sleeper" regarded those primeval human forms that were fertilized, not by their like, but from their environment. Before the sick person who lay in the temple sleep stood the form of she who bore her kind without being fertilized by her kind. Before such a person stood she who brings forth the woman with the child, the Virgin Goddess who, in the Lemurian epoch, was the companion of humankind but had since disappeared from human sight—called the holy Isis in ancient Egypt. Isis could normally be seen by people in those times only before death came to the world. In normal consciousness, people were then companions of such figures who hovered about them, and they brought forth their kind immaculately.

The priests said that, when Isis was no longer the visible companion of humanity—once she was withdrawn into the circle of the Gods—she continued her interest, through the spiritual world, in the health of humankind. And when the vision of those ancient figures, the Isis image, was brought to a human being in an abnormal way (as in the temple sleep), the goddess remained a means of healing, for she is the principle in human beings that was present in them before mortal sheaths enveloped human beings. No mortal had lifted her veil, for she was present when death had not yet come into the world. Rooted in the eternal, she is the great healer, the being whom humanity will reach again when humankind returns to spiritual wisdom.

We can experience something of what remains of this—the wonderful symbol of the virgin mother. From the view of spiritual science, it can certainly be emphasized that the picture has a healing effect. When it is contemplated in such a way that it has an aftereffect on the human soul—for instance, when the soul lies in sleep and can dream of this picture—it has a healing effect to this very day.[7]

The Madonna and child image is much older than we imagine:

Writing, in its beginning, was a kind of imitation, a representation of the universe by vision, by images. There were pictures of everything visible as well as invisible to our sense organs. There were pictures for the elements fire, water, earth, metals, for the heaven, the Sun, Moon and stars, for mountains and fields, for rain and sunshine, light and darkness, morning and evening, a living man and a corpse, for mother and father, infant, son, and daughter. Little by little, even the most complex ideas...could be represented by images.

As long as Chinese artists-writers used their original pictures with their great artistic talent and fine technical skills, everyone could read them easily....

Love was symbolized by a compound sign consisting of mother and child, the same symbol as the Madonna of the Catholic Church.[8]

Since ancient times, cults of all kinds have been dedicated to this great Mother. Apart from cave paintings, figures of the great Mother represent the oldest works of art and religion that we know. The well-known Venus of Willendorf, a distended, swelling female figure, was created roughly 22,000 years before Christ. In those cults, which were dedicated to the great Mother, mothers were active as priestesses.[9]

---

[7] Rudolf Steiner, *Universe, Earth and Man: In Their Relationship to Egyptian Myths and Modern Civilization* (London: Rudolf Steiner Press, 1987), pp. 12–31 (trans. revised).

[8] Arnold D. Wadler, *One Language: Source of All Tongues* (Great Barrington, MA: Lindisfarne Books, 2006), pp. 58–61.

[9] Manfred Schmidt-Brabant and Virginia Sease, *The Archetypal Feminine in the Mystery Stream of Humanity: Towards a New Culture of the Family* (London: Temple Lodge, 1999), p. 49.

I focused on the eyes and the eye contact between the Madonna and the child or with the other figures, and how they looked at the Jesus child. One can see enormous love pouring from those expressive looks and how they were painted with such adoration. And one could see how the tourists' faces were softened as they looked at these ancient masterpieces. It reminds me of Georg Kühlewind's comments on joy:

> In the human sphere, joy appears in manifold colors and under equally manifold conditions. The adult human being knows mainly those joys that are caused by outer or inner conditions, with a gradual transition on a continuous scale to enjoyments and pleasures of soul and body. However, in the young child one can experience other joys, which appear along with the faculty of speaking. Speaking begins with the encounter and meeting of glances between the child and the adult, which is a unique experience in its quality and remains so for the entire life; no other object receives such a look, that kind of seeing, as the look into the eye of a human being. Details are not seen—often one hardly remembers the color of the eye one has looked into, because it is the speaking essence of the human being that talks to us through the glance of the eye, what we address with our look.
>
> The next stage in the process of learning to speak is the mutual smiling of the child and adult. This smile is the sign of joy; it is joy itself—joy about the beginning of a dialogue, the participation in the community of human beings. Therefore, in the animal kingdom one cannot find the glance of the human eye, nor the smile. The child finds joy in the experience of word-nature, initially in looks and smiles.[10]

After so many hundreds of years, these Madonna paintings still have the ability to transform someone's soul.

I moved on to the Botticelli room. He is one of my favorite painters. Sandro Botticelli's *Birth of Venus* had hundreds of admirers. Love coming to the earthly realm—love coming into being using ancient images, cosmic happenings, which coincides with chivalry and courtly love, the *Roman de la rose*. In ancient times, there was no question of love between human beings. With this painting, which has acquired world fame, love comes into the world with a certain elegance and beauty. Everyone is fascinated by it there in the room. Whether Japanese, French, or any other culture, people are intrigued by this image of Venus, or Love. The metal for the planet Venus is copper, whose

---

10 Georg Kühlewind, "Thinking with the Heart" (private publication), p. 60.

function as we know is to be a great medium for warmth. In the painting, she sits on a shell, which floats on a copper-green sea. Perhaps standing on the shell might be a symbol of the pearl/love acquired at the expense of suffering. A wind blows her to the shore, where a flowery young woman will dress her in a soft, flowery red, silky veil, to welcome Love/Venus to Earth. Rudolf Steiner said this about Botticelli's *Venus:*

> We know that it harms us to exert ourselves with too much "I" activity. This is easy to understand because "I" activity is, after all, a breaking-down process. If too much disintegration takes place, our organism is clearly and visibly weakened. We can notice this visible weakening at first glance. But there can also be a weakening of our etheric body through the astral body, since the latter can excessively deplete, so to speak, our etheric body. The most common symptom of this kind occurs when we live in a way that demands too much of our astral body—the vehicle of our passions and emotions. As you know, such a lifestyle can lead to permanent weakening. Such impairment results from the astral body depleting the etheric body....
>
> Whether we have a tendency to develop strong emotions and passions in our astral body is of course connected with our karma. These passions, however, can be, in a way, humanly significant and meaningful. For example, consider a quality that plays a role throughout human life and is nevertheless a passion, albeit the noblest passion, one that in its noblest form can develop into freedom from selfishness—love. Love is a passion, but it can become entirely free of egotism. It is the only passion that can become free of egotism. It is located in the astral body, which is its vehicle.
>
> Let us assume that an artist with a true feeling for reality has been given the task to create a human form suffused and permeated throughout with the passion of love, the noble passion of love. Clearly, such an artist could not be a naturalist, since naturalists have no feeling for realities, but see only abstract, "naturalist" matter—so-called actuality. Every time artists had the task of creating a Venus, or Aphrodite, they had to feel that the figure would have to be completely suffused by the passion of love. Love must be abundant and must pour itself out. Consequently, then, the astral body of Aphrodite, or Venus, cannot be like any other female astral body, otherwise every woman and girl would be an Aphrodite or a Venus—and that is not the case, is it? This means it is a special development of the astral body. The artist does not have to know anything about spiritual science but must feel through creating a

Venus that her astral body must be more strongly developed than that of a non-Aphrodite, or non-Venus.

However, as we have said, the astral body has a depleting consuming nature. This has to be expressed in the work of art. How will the artist who really feels this, who really has a sense for the depleting astral body, set about creating a Venus? One will have to show that there is something about the physical body that gradually consumes it....

Suppose an artist had created a Venus. While creating her, the artist feels correctly that she had a more strongly consuming and depleting astral body than any other woman. We will see this in the slender neck and the shape of the chest. We will also see in other parts of the body that, basically, her astral body has a depleting nature. If the artist gives the matter physical expression, perhaps we will see in her overall shape that she will not live to a very old age. When one achieves such a creation, spiritual science will say the artist has a sense for the underlying reality....

However, what will a physician say (especially one who is not a spiritual scientist) when he sees such a figure created by an artist? He will say, "This represents a person suffering from tuberculosis." Indeed, people who suffer from tuberculosis also have a more strongly consuming and depleting astral body...than do other people. Most of you know that Botticelli has painted a most beautiful and wonderful Venus. In his picture of Venus standing on a shell, we see a physical body painted in such a way that we cannot help thinking it is based on a depleting astral body. That is why art historians disagree about this painting. Some of them admire the figure of this Venus precisely for its deviation from the so-called normal human form; they admire her slender neck and the unusual shape of her upper chest, and so forth. Others say these features are the result of Botticelli having painted a model who suffered from tuberculosis.

Well, it is certainly possible to explain everything in a materialistic way. It is likely that Botticelli actually did paint a model with tuberculosis—specifically, Simonetta [Cattaneo de Vespucci], who died at the age of twenty-three. But that is not the point. What is important is that he knew he wanted precisely this woman to sit for his *Venus*.[11]

Sandro Botticelli (c.1445–1510) was born in Florence and painted in the studio of Lippi and circulated in the Medician world of Florence. Around 1477, he became part of a team that frescoed biblical scenes in the Sistine Chapel.

---

11 Rudolf Steiner, *Toward Imagination: Culture and the Individual* (Hudson, NY: Anthroposophic Press, 1990), p. 80–82 (translation revised).

When he returned to Florence, his work in Rome had enhanced his prestige as an artist. Lorenzo di Pierfrancesco de' Medici became a regular patron of Botticelli, and it is likely that he painted *Primavera* and *The Birth of Venus* for him. Nevertheless, despite his enormous achievements, Botticelli died abandoned and alone.

In the great room, I snatched a little corner on a bench, so that I could admire *La Primavera*. The enormous masterpiece is more than beautiful; it has an aura of mystery in it. The subject is not obvious, but immersed in mystery knowledge. The details refer to great moments in human history. Everything is allegorical, and one must understand the ancient language of mystery knowledge to grasp it.

Scholars and artists continue to argue over what the paintings mean—that it depicts Venus' arrival on the Earth or that love is born or that it is springtime for humanity. The strong wind and undressed goddess; a barefoot flower princess; Venus dressed with a red shawl and with a bush of myrtle (her sacred plant); the three graces (or three aspects of the soul—thinking, feeling, willing); and Mercury, the healer with his caduceus—all these intended to be absorbed in a meditative mood. The effect of these paintings on the admirer is one of being stunned. It comes from realms not of this world, and requires us to build a bridge between the Heaven and the Earth to understand them. It is nevertheless clear that we human beings did not arise from apes. It offers an alternative to a Darwinian interpretation of human history, one from the realm of the Gods.

Otherwise, the great Boticelli would have painted a scene full of apes, climbing trees and engaging in natural behavior. And we would have called these our forefathers and our souls would not be so uplifted, but rather the opposite.

> Darwinism has made many errors in regard to the differentiation expressed by the races [species] existing on Earth. The higher races have not descended from the lower races; on the contrary, the latter represent the degeneration of the higher races that preceded them. Suppose there are two brothers, one of whom is handsome and intelligent, the other ugly and dull. Both proceed from the same father. What should we think of those who believed that the intelligent brother descends from the idiot? This is the kind of error Darwinism makes in regard to the races. Human and animal have a common origin; animals represent a degeneration of a single common ancestor, whose higher development is expressed in the human being. This should be a

source of pride, since the higher races have been able to develop only because of the lower kingdoms.

Christ washes the feet of the Apostles. This is a symbol of the humility of the initiate in the face of inferiors. Initiates owe their existence to those who are not initiated. Hence the deep humility of those who truly know in face of those who do not. The tragic aspect of cosmic evolution is that one class of beings must lower themselves so that the other may rise....

Just as humankind has wrested itself from the animal, likewise humankind will wrest itself from evil. But never before has humanity passed through a crisis as severe as that of the present age. Evil and goodness remain within human beings; similarly, in the past animals were within humankind. The aim of Manicheism is to sublimate human beings to become redeemers.

The Master must be the servant of all.[12]

Viewing these *chef-d'œuvres,* one becomes aware of another fact: there are too many paintings. One would be enough to study for a whole week. It is too much for the eyes. So many paintings are not meant to be in a single large room...much better to show them one-by-one and admire them individually. They should not be thrown together in enormous rooms with no time or space to meditate on their beauty. Nevertheless, we all did our best to admire such great paintings.

We stood riveted to Leonardo's paintings at the Uffizi. *The Adoration of the Magi,* is an unfinished painting, left in monochromatic tones that reveal the virtuosity of the drawing style and composition. *The Baptism of Christ,* a work by Verrocchio, who asked his young student Leonardo to paint in an angel, exudes unearthly strength in the figures of Christ and John the Baptist.

There was also an exhibition on Leornardo da Vinci. We have not yet realized the depth of his knowledge, never mind trying to understand it. His mind soared far above ours and it seems it will for hundreds of years to come. For me as a linguist, what was fascinating in this special exhibition was the explanation of his language. Some drawings represent words that could be put together. His own sign–symbol–word language shows to me that words were not dead to him. He was able to experience living language; words were not dead and abstract, but alive and full of spiritual content. He was able to read

---

12 Rudolf Steiner, *An Esoteric Cosmology: Evolution, Christ & Modern Spirituality* (Great Barrington, MA: SteinerBooks, 2008), pp. 9–10.

the book of life, which is mute for us unless we are serious about a meditation practice to develop our soul faculties. Part of the exhibition was a deep study of *The Last Supper*. I was riveted to the screen explaining the different gestures of the twelve apostles, their hand positions, their faces, what each apostle felt when faced with Christ's statement, "One of you will betray me."

A book that does justice to his work is *Leonardo da Vinci: The Last Supper* by Michael Ladwein. It is a deep, scholarly study of Leonardo's painting in which this quote appears:

> When Leonardo wanted to paint a person in a picture he first considered that individual's characteristics and qualities: was he noble or vulgar, cheerful or stern, somber or joyful, old or young, irascible or calm, good or bad. Having grown to understand his nature he then frequented places where people of that kind were in the habit of gathering. With care he observed the faces, their behavior, their garments and bodily movements. And when he found something that might be useful for his purposes he recorded it with his draftsman's pencil in a little book he always carried attached to his belt. Having done this many times and gathered what seemed sufficient material for his project he then set to work and made a wonderfully successful painting. Assuming that he also did this for every work he created, he must have done it also with the greatest care for the picture he painted in the monastery of the Order of the Preachers in which our Savior is depicted seated at table with his disciples. (Giovanbatista Giraldi)[13]

In La Galleria degli Uffizi, I move on through the various rooms and stop in front of Raphael's *Madonna of the Goldfinch* (1505) to absorb its serene beauty. As we continue our walk through the galleries and try to take in the hundreds of paintings, people tend to pause in front of what touches their souls. Although we are marched along like cattle, there is nonetheless a certain mood. People are awed and speechless. They are transported into other worlds, away from everyday earthly experiences.

> To a certain extent, the aesthetic human rises above the stream of development and enters a different world. And that is important. The aesthetically inclined person and the person who works in an aesthetic field do not act in a way that is entirely appropriate to someone on

---

13 Michael Ladwein, *Leonardo da Vinci: The Last Supper: A Cosmic Drama and an Act of Redemption* (London: Temple Lodge, 2006), p. 42.

Earth; rather their sphere of activity is in a certain way lifted out of the Earth sphere. With this discovery, aesthetics leads us to some profound secret of human existence.

On the one hand, anyone who expresses such things as these is touching on the highest truths; on the other, what such a one says can sound virtually nonsensical—mad and distorted. But we will never understand life as long as we timidly hold ourselves back from the real truths. Take any work of art that you wish—the *Sistine Madonna* or the *Venus de Milo*. If it really is a work of art, it is not entirely of this Earth. It has been lifted out of the stream of earthly events. That is self-evident. And what lives in a *Sistine Madonna* or a *Venus de Milo*? What lives in them also lives in the human being. It is a power not entirely adapted to Earth. If everything in humanity were adapted to the Earth, humankind would not be able to live on any other level. But not everything in the human being is adapted to the Earth and, for esoteric vision, not everything in humanity is attuned to being human on Earth. There are mysterious forces that some day will provide humanity with the impetus to lift itself out of the sphere of earthly existence. Nor will we ever understand art as such until we see that its task is to point beyond the merely earthly and beyond what is solely adapted to Earth—to point to the sphere where that which lives in the *Venus de Milo* truly does exist....

What is merely logical is not necessarily valid; only what measures up to reality is valid.... We need philosophers who are not satisfied to limit themselves to their powers of abstractions, thinking up new abstractions. More and increasingly more, thinking must arise that accords with reality and is not merely logical. Thinking alters the whole course of world evolution. For what is a *Venus de Milo* or a *Sistine Madonna* from the view of thinking that accords with reality? If you take them merely at face value, you are not in contact with reality. You must be enraptured. To truly see a work of art, you must be lifted out of the Earth's sphere and removed from it. To really encounter the *Venus de Milo,* your soul must be different from the soul that responds to earthly things; precisely the things that do not exist on this earthly plane are what transport the soul to the plane where they really do exist—to the realm of the elemental world, which is where what is in the *Venus de Milo* really exists. One is able to stand before that painting in a way that accords with reality precisely because she possesses the power to tear us away from mere sense bound vision....

What would happen if there were no art in the world? If that were so, all the forces that are now devoted to art and the enjoyment of art would be used to produce a life that runs counter to reality. If you were to remove art from the development of humanity, then human development would contain just as many lies as it now contains works of art....

Truly aesthetic human behavior involves enlivening the sensory organs and ensouling of the life processes. This is an extremely important truth about humanity; it explains much. Enlivening the sensory organs and a new life in the realms of the senses is found in the arts and in the enjoyment of art. Something similar occurs with the vital processes, which are more ensouled in the enjoyment of art than they are in normal life. These days, it is impossible to understand the full significance of the changes a person undergoes when entering the artistic realm, because a materialistic approach is incapable of grasping the facts in full reality....

The artist must go through a process whereby the "I" is lifted out of the specialization acquired on Earth; it must give us a generalized sense of meaning, a sense of the typical. Artists do this as a matter of course. Similarly, artists cannot directly express the world of thoughts in the way it is usually expressed here on Earth. Otherwise they would be unable to produce poetry or works of art, or at the most only didactic works that contain some lesson, but are not artistic in the true sense of the word.[14]

I spend six hours walking through the galleries before feeling compelled to leave and regain my senses. Goethe had this to say of his travels in Italy:

As I rush through Rome looking at the major monuments the immensity of the place has a quietening effect. In other places one has to search for the important points of interest; here they crowd in on one in profusion. Wherever you turn your eyes, every kind of vista, near and distant, confronts you—palaces, ruins, gardens, wildernesses, small houses, stables, triumphal arches, columns—all of them often so close together that they could be sketched on a single sheet of paper.... And then in the evening, one feels exhausted after so much looking and admiring.[15]

Back on the streets, I notice the young girls in their scanty clothes; it seems they might as well be naked. Not to worry; fashion will probably change and they will cover up again. Here is Beppe Severgnini's observations on the situation:

The new Italian icon is the Semi-Undressed Signorina. We ought to put her on coins and stamps. Her face is interchangeable, but from the neck down everything stays the same. She turns up in every TV program,

---

14 Rudolf Steiner, *The Riddle of Humanity,* pp. 124–128 (translation revised).
15 Goethe, *Italian Journey* (New York: Penguin Books, 1970), p. 133.

wiggles her hips, and every so often gets to speak, especially when she has nothing to say....

We are not talking about some den of corruption. We're talking about a country that went straight from chronic inhibition to uninterrupted titillation....

Look at this evening's commercials. There are dozens of products advertised through sexual imagery or allusions—aftershave, air conditioning, antitheft devices, aperitifs, automobiles, bananas, beer, biscuits, cell phones, chocolates, chronometers, coffee, deodorants, dishwashing liquid, divans, and duvets. And that's only up to the letter "d." [16]

Tomorrow I am off to Siena for the day. More amazing riches await in that famous little city. I am so busy visiting museums, churches, old buildings, and so on that I have no time to do what I originally intended, which is write. I am having a hard time writing about what has happened while there is so much to see and live in the present. I have to leave quite early and not oversleep, otherwise I will miss the early train, which leaves from the center of town. Nevertheless, I am happy not to be staying inside the city.

It is very peaceful up in this hill town of Settignano not far from Florence, with its beautiful Tuscan villas, olive trees, cypresses, and soft hills. It soothes the eyes after the busy streets of Florence. Cypress trees line some of the narrow streets, and other evergreens shape the horizon into pleasant panoramas. Of course one can see the steeples of old churches and monasteries dotting the hillside, along with numerous olive trees ripening under the warm September sun. People are in their gardens and orchards, enjoying the fruits of their labor. I can barely hear the families arguing with their teenagers from their opened windows. The many immigrants return home on the buses after a day of housework in the villas, while others rush home on their Vespas. After a day's work in Florence, people are ready to enjoy the warm evening. People rush to the small local store for last-minute supplies of fresh pesto sauce or some nice grapes, a salami, local wine, fresh

---

16 Beppe Severgnini, *La Bella Figura*, pp. 77–78.

pasta, olives. Others sit at the local café to sip an aperitif and chat with friends before going home.

I must call my daughter to see what she is up to. After life in the Midwest, she has fallen in love with life in Spain and with a young Italian man. She claims that we deprived her by living on the farm.

It is quiet now. It's a good time to go for a stroll in the olive orchard and eat a few figs before they all disappear.

I took the early train and reached Siena ahead of the crowds. The train was full of tourists and kids headed to school, but I watched the countryside more than I did my fellow passengers, many of whom were using cell phones.

> The astonishing popularity of cell phones in Italy is not due simply to convenience. The new toy also ticks a whole series of boxes in the national character.
>
> The phenomenon started out as a way of showing off (I've got one, what about you?). Then cell phone became token of belonging ("Have you got one?" "Me, too!"). Finally, they were viewed as a necessity ("We've all got one. Couldn't live without them!").
>
> Today's success hinges on the tentacular nature of the Italian family. The Finns own proportionately more cell phones than we do. They'd be happy to use them all the time, but they don't know who to call. We Italians know only too well. Pop calls Mom, Mom calls son, son calls friend, friend calls other friend from the office, other friend calls casual acquaintance, casual acquaintance calls girlfriend, girlfriend calls sister, sister calls her folks, folks ring uncle and aunt, uncle and aunt call nephews and nieces, nephews and nieces ring home, Mom answers, and then calls Pop who is standing in line at the bank. The circle is complete. They can start again.[17]

I walked up to the old town, a nice three-mile walk, while everyone else took the bus. I though it would be a smaller town. I can see why Siena tried to compete with Florence during the Middle Ages. The churches here are

---

17 Beppe Severgnini, *La Bella Figura*, p. 112.

Siena and Piazza del Campo (lower left)

outstanding and filled with the beautiful, priceless early paintings I love. I always pass by the other paintings, but I am mesmerized by these early jewels of the Madonna and child. Again, I took many pictures, even where it was forbidden. To me, they are too precious to let them go without having some remembrance of those gentle, quiet, dignified, and beautiful faces.

One can easily partake in the Marian cult here. There are countless little niches and small sanctuaries in the big churches or cathedrals where one can sit quietly and pray or just sit in contemplation. These little corners of the bigger churches are often busier than the main parts of the cathedral. They provide small, safe havens for the faithful in an otherwise large, impersonal space.

Hundreds of tourists flock to these ancient places of worship. Il Duomo di Siena, dedicated to Santa Maria Assunta (Holy Mary of Assumption), is one of these great Cathedrals. People from around the world pass by, but they seem bewildered, unable to understand what they are seeing, whether angels, archangels, or apostles. The images are overwhelming and monumental.

Georg Kühlewind (1924–2006), a Hungarian scientist, a professor and Greek scholar fluent in several languages, a master of meditation, and deeply Christian, speaks of angels this way:

> We must take seriously the names of the angels and archangels—if we were only capable of understanding them! For the words have lost their original and primal meaning for us; only in meditation can one sometimes enter their inner space, their *sancrum,* for a tiny spark of understanding. Gabriel—God's Hero; Raphael—God heals; Uriel—Gods Light; Samuel—God listens; Orifiel—Light from Gods' mouth; Azael—God's power. Who dares to look behind the sound of the word, which through its glaring surface strictly turns the unexperienced away? The name of the Spirit of the Time, Michael, is a question: Who is as God?... He is the only Divinity that carries a question for a name.... Compared to a statement, a question means: permeability, searching, to be on the way—in the name of Michael, and all of this in the name of God. It is an eternal quest, directed a the highest aim. One can avoid a human question, but not one that is a being. He who meets this question is forced by the might of an archangel and archai; "Reflect on yourself! Know thyself!"[18]

One is stunned by the way people walk amid these powerful paintings and sculptures without really understanding any of it. How could we? Our task is elsewhere. Kühlewind tells us:

> Behind the saying "God is dead" is the experience that the Godhead is now silent: Without a contribution—questioning—on the part of the human, the Godhead is no longer given. Humankind must begin: "Ask, seek, and knock" (Matt. 7:7) Then Michael, the Spirit of the Times, the divinity that is waiting for his step, his beginning, can offer help.
>
> In His silent way of expectation, the Spirit of the Times directs human striving upward, above the languages, in the direction of the creative, "wordless words." In relation to the word of a language, the wordless word is to be found in the opposite direction of abstract thinking, which has separated itself from the language.[19]

Pico della Mirandola (1463–1494), a philosopher of the Florentine platonic school, helps us come a bit closer to the great and powerful archangelic beings:

---

18 Georg Kühlewind, "Thinking of the Heart," p. 36.
19 Ibid., p. 38.

And if it is right, to bring into the open anything at all of the occult mysteries, even in the guise of a riddle, since a sudden fall from heaven has condemned the head of man to dizziness, and, in the words of Jeremiah, death has come in through our windows and smitten our vitals and our heart; let us summon Raphael, celestial physician, that he may set us free by moral philosophy and by dialectic as though by wholesome drugs. Then, when we are restored to health, Gabriel, "strength of God," shall abide in us, leading us through the miracles of nature and showing us on every side the merit and the might of God. He will at last consign us to the high priest Michael, who will distinguish those who have completed their term in the service of philosophy with the holy office of theology as if with a crown of precious stones.[20]

Even now as I walk every day in these sumptuous houses of the Lord, the images, paintings, sculptures remain an enigma to me as well as to everyone else, especially to the ones who try to explain these sacred works of Christian art with abstract words, but reading words from great men such as Pico della Mirandola certainly helps. But in these sacred paintings we truly have a universal language.

The only ones who speak an international, universal language are the Madonna and child paintings. They speak to all, no matter the religious denomination; every one sits quietly, impregnating the world of non-word communication that unites us with the great all. Invariably, I stand next to these sacred icons or just sit, trying to live in the realm of universal love, care, unselfishness, tenderness, and motherhood that lives in the painting, because that love was so alive in the hearts of the medieval painters. And of course it still lives in women who carry a child and in the men who welcome them.

Raphael, Leonardo, and Dante were all imbued with a culture that teemed with sense and meaning, a culture that filled and surrounded the souls of human beings. There was a profound reason why Raphael painted Madonnas. The essence of the Madonna lived in human hearts and souls, and in the very highest sense something streamed from the soul of the public and flowed toward the creations of these great artists. When Dante set out to transport the human soul into spiritual realms, he merely had to draw his material from something that was resounding

---

20 Pico della Mirandola, *Oration on the Dignity of Man* (1486), available at www.cscs.umich.edu/~crshalizi/Mirandola.

The grand interior of the Duomo dell'Assunta, Siena

Paintings in Opera del Duomo Museum in Siena

in every soul. These artists possessed in their own souls the substance of the culture of their respective time.

In any work belonging to the culture of its own time, however obscure, we shall find connecting links with an element that was living in all human souls, right down to the humblest circles. The scholars in the cultural environment out of which Raphael created his madonnas, were themselves thoroughly imbued with the idea of the Madonna. In this sense, artistic creations appear as expressions of the general, homogeneous culture of their time....

During the epochs of great art, the content of art is immediately perceptible because it flows from something that moves the innermost human being.[21]

After lingering in various churches and museums, I walk the tiny sinuous, climbing streets of Siena to savor a cup of cappuccino accompanied by local nutty pastries and a view of the passers by. What a myriad of faces—all beautiful, coming to share a sunny Tuscany day.

I helped myself to some figs and walked back to the train station for my return to Florence. I saw numerous tall, ebony Africans boarding the train, all seeming to have a story to tell from their homeland. I love listening to Africans speaking their language. It is full of life, not Latinized—in other words, not deadened by tightly structured grammar. I can still feel the pulse of life through lovely, warm vowels, accompanied by lots of *m*'s and *b*'s, making it almost motherly. It subtly conveys a feel of the African sun, smiling in the quiet train ride home.

My daughter will fly from Barcelona for a week, which will coincide with October 4, the feast day of Francis of Assisi. She was born on my birthday October 3, which makes it a good time to visit the ancient site of one of my favorite Christian saints.

After viewing so many paintings of Madonna and child for two weeks, I am drawn to the looks that lovers give each other, especially the young people. It is that look of tenderness and affection that it seems one doesn't see so much in the U.S. In the Midwest, one rarely sees young people being loving toward each other. But here in Germany, Spain, and Italy, I have noticed that young people are very sweet to each other. Perhaps this is why I see so

---

21 Rudolf Steiner, *Architecture as a Synthesis of the Arts* (London: Rudolf Steiner Press, 1999), pp. 134–135.

many American young girls and boys walking everywhere here in Europe. My own daughter explained that this is something she enjoys about living in Barcelona; men are not bashful about showing their feelings.

Rudolf Steiner had this to say about love:

> Phenomena that appear one way in our physical world look quite different in the higher, spiritual world. One might even say that the gods profit from that participation in human life. We must try to master a difficult but necessary concept if we are to understand the relationship of humanity to the universe. We have said that the Earth is the planet of love and that love will be developed in its true form first on Earth. To put it bluntly, love will be bred here, and through their participation in human life the gods will come to know love just as, in another sense, it is they whose gift it is. It is a difficult concept.
>
> It is entirely possible for one being to impart a gift to another and yet come to gain knowledge of it only through the other. Picture a very wealthy man who has never known anything but riches and has never experienced the deep satisfaction of soul that good deeds can bring. Now picture this person performing a good deed by giving to the poor. The gift evokes gratitude in the soul of the needy recipient, and this feeling of gratitude is at the same time a gift; it would not exist had not the wealthy person first made the gift. Although he does not feel it, the wealthy man is the originator of that feeling of gratitude. He can come to know it once it is reflected back from the individual in whom he has aroused that feeling. To some extent, this resembles the way the gods impart love to human beings. They have reached the stage at which they can kindle love in human beings so that the gods learn to experience it, but they themselves can become acquainted with it, as a reality, only through the human being. Leaving their heights, the gods submerge themselves in the ocean of humanity and feel the warmth of love. We know that the gods are deprived of something if human lives lack love, and that, in a sense, they find nourishment in the love that prevails among human beings. The more human love there is on Earth, the more food there is for the gods in Heaven; the less there is love, the more the gods go hungry.
>
> Humankind's offering to the gods is really nothing but the love that flows up to them—the love generated in human beings.[22]

And here is love seen from another perspective:

---
22 Rudolf Steiner, *Universe, Earth, and Man*, pp. 124-125.

The Earth has been "mineralized," as has the human physical body. But the characteristic feature of human beings is the twofold movement that takes places in them. As physical beings, humans have descended; as spiritual beings, we have ascended. St. Paul spoke of this truth when he declared that there is one law for the body and another for the spirit. Thus the human being represents both an end and a beginning.

The vital point, that of intersection and change in the ascending life of humankind, is also the separation of the sexes. There was an age when the two sexes were united in the human being. Even Darwin recognized this as a probability. Because of the separation of the sexes, a new, all-embracing element arose: love. The attraction of love is so powerful and mysterious that when tropical butterflies of different sexes are moved to Europe and then released into the air, they will fly back again and meet each other halfway.

There is some analogy between the relations established by the human world with the divine world and by the human kingdom with the animal kingdom. Oxygen and carbon dioxide are inhaled and exhaled by human beings. The plant kingdom breathes out oxygen; the human kingdom breathes out love since the separation of the sexes. The gods are nourished by this effluence of love.

How is it that animals and human beings exhale love? In humanity today, esotericists see beings in the full swing of evolution. Human beings are both fallen gods and gods becoming. The kingdom of the heavens is nourished by the effluence of human love. Ancient Greek mythology expresses this fact when it speaks of nectar and ambrosia. The gods are so far above human beings that their natural tendency would be to subjugate them. But there is a halfway state of being between humans and the gods, just as the mistletoe is halfway between plant and animal. It is represented by Lucifer and the luciferic element. The interest of the gods is the element of human love, through which their life is sustained.[23]

Another day in Florence. This time I visited of my favorites, the Museum of San Marco and the cloister. It was free for a change, and of course cameras

---

23 Rudolf Steiner, *An Esoteric Cosmology*, pp. 13–14.

Certosa del Galluzzo Cistercian cloisters

are not allowed. But I managed to take quite a few pictures of the remarkable frescoes. Some of the most amazing works I've seen, the frescoes have a somber, quiet presence, with a virgin-like quality. The use of color shows deep knowledge. I did not stay long in the cells where the paintings were too bloody, at times depicting extreme asceticism. The simplicity of design and form, along with exquisite details of the robes and a frugal use of gold adds to the power of the works. Most powerful is the use of indigo, which would be used even more powerfully in Spain by El Greco in his haunting paintings. The greens are light and translucent, the color *Caput mortuum* (also known as "cardinal purple," a brownish liver color) adds another dimension to the Pieta scenes. The frescoes seemed to me very modern in design, almost geometrical, with a bold use of colors that plunge the viewer, and the monks for whom they were painted, into a state of deep meditation. Most powerful are the scenes of the Anunciation, the Pietas, the deep sorrow of Magdalene clothed in a vermilion robe in the Pieta, the last supper, and many others. Many of the cells have frescoes of the Crucifixion, one of which was Girolamo Savonarola's cell.

Fra Giovanni Angelico was born in the North of Florence in 1387 and took his vows at the Monastery San Domenico in Fiesole around 1418. In 1438, he went to the convent of San Marco in Florence and obtained the work of decorating the convent. He was trained in the late Gothic manner and influenced by the illumination and gold work of northern Europe. Fra Angelico worked throughout Italy, in Rome at the Vatican, in Orvieto at the Cathedral, and in Florence. He died in Rome in 1455.

After such a powerful few hours, I went for a walk and got lost as usual. I just turn here then there and see where I end up. I came upon the chapel where Dante met Beatrice, so I took a few pictures. It was moving to sit there knowing that so many others have found inspiration here. To imagine that this bigger-than-life human being walked here so many years ago. The thought was almost too big for comprehension. I had to sit quietly and just breathe. If not for lovely Beatrice, we would not have Dante's *Divine Comedy*.

> When you follow the teaching of the Templars, there at its heart is a kind of reverence for something of a feminine nature. This femininity was known as the Divine Sophia, the Heavenly Wisdom. *Manas* is the fifth principle, the human spiritual self that must be developed, for which a temple must be built. And just as the pentagon at the entrance to Solomon's Temple characterizes the fivefold human being (da Vinci's famous drawing), the female principle similarly typifies the wisdom of the Middle Ages. This wisdom is exactly what Dante sought to personify in his Beatrice. Dante's *Divine Comedy* can be understood only from this viewpoint. Hence, you find Dante, too, using the symbols that find expression through the Templars, the Christian knights of the Grail, and so on.[24]

What peculiar names—*divine* and *comedy*. But what could we call life if not a comedy, all of it based on the beautiful Beatrice, or love? The ideal beauty aids in our ascent back to the divine. In all of this, is woman supposed to be only the ideal, something that can never be reached? Are we as women supposed to entice men by our beauty and nothing else? Between the ideal lover, which men look up to, and the virgin mother of the child, is there room for anything else? All the young women—whom do they have to look up to on Earth? Remain forever the lover until youth is no longer, become mothers, and then what?

---

24 Rudolf Steiner, *The Temple Legend*, p. 145.

The Annunciation *(c. 1440)*, Fra Angelico
(fresco in a monk's cell, San Marco Museum)

Vladimir Solovyov is the only writer I've encountered who offers answers. He tries to bring women to a level other than that of holy Virgin or the unattainable, ideal lover: the union of man and woman. In his book, *The Meaning of Love*,[25] he offers his views on love:

> We know that a human beings, in addition to animal material nature, possess an ideal nature that binds them with absolute truth, or with God. Besides the material or empirical content of life, human beings comprise the image of God, a special form of the absolute content. Theoretically, and in the abstract, this Divine image is known to us in the concrete and in life. And if this revelation of the ideal being, ordinarily concealed by its material manifestation, is not limited in love to merely an internal feeling, but at times becomes noticeable also in the sphere of external feelings, then so much greater is the significance we must acknowledge for love, as being from the very beginning the visible restoration of the Divine image in the material world, the beginning of the embodiment of true ideal humanity. The power of love, passing into the world, transforming and spiritualizing the form of external phenomena, reveals to us its objective might, and after that it is up to us. We ourselves must understand this revelation and take advantage of it so that it may not remain a passing enigmatic flash of some mystery.
>
> The psycho-physical process of restoring the Divine image in material humanity has no means of perfecting itself on its own and apart from us. Its origin, like that of everything better in this world, arises from the realm of unconscious processes in relations obscure to us. There lie the germ and root of the tree of life, but we must foster it with our conscious activity. For the beginning, passive receptivity of feeling suffices, but subsequently active faith is necessary, along with moral effort and hard work, to keep for oneself, to strengthen and develop this gift of luminous and creative love, in order through it to incarnate in oneself and in another the image of God, and to create out of two infinite and perishable natures one absolute and immortal individuality. If, inevitably and without our own volition, the existent idealization of love reveals to us, through empirical appearance, a distant ideal image of the beloved object, this is not of course, only that we might delight in it, but also that, by power of true faith, active imagination and real creativeness we might transform in accordance with this true exemplar the reality not corresponding to it, and might embody it in a real phenomenon.... (pp. 60–61)

---

25 Vladimir Solovyov, *The Meaning of Love* (Great Barrington, MA: Lindisfarne Books, 1985).

The feeling of love in itself is only an impulse, suggesting to us that we can and should restore the integrity of the human being. Each time this sacred spark is kindled in a human heart, all of creation waits groaning and travailing for the first revelation of the glory of the sons of God. But without the activity of the conscious human spirit, the Divine spark is extinguished, and deceived nature creates new generations of the sons of men for new hope.... (pp. 64–65)

This true idea of the beloved object, though it shines through the real phenomenon in the instant of love's intense emotion [the Divine Spark], is at first manifested in a clearer aspect only as the object of imagination. The concrete form of this imagination, the ideal image in which I clothe the beloved person at the given moment, is of course created by me, but it is not created out of nothing. And the subjectivity of this image as such—i.e, as it manifests itself here and now before the eyes of my soul—by no means proves that it is subjective, or a characteristic of an imaginary object that exists for me alone. If for me, who am myself on this side of the transcendental world, a certain ideal object appears to be only the product of my own imagination, this does not interfere with its full reality in another higher sphere of being. And though our real life is outside this higher sphere, yet our mind is not wholly alien to it, and we can possess a certain abstract comprehension of the laws of its being. And here is the first basic law: If in our world, separate and isolated existence is a fact and an actuality while unity is only a concept and an idea, then in the higher sphere, by contrast, reality appertains to the unity or, more accurately, to the unity-of-the-all, while separateness and individualization exist only potentially and subjectively.

From this it follows that the being of *this* person in the transcendental sphere is not an individual one, in the sense of a real being in this world. There, in the truth, the individual person is only a living and real yet indivisible ray of one ideal light—the unity-of-the-all essence. This ideal person, or personified idea, is only an individualization of the unity-of-the-all, which is indivisibly present in each of its individualizations. So, when we imagine the ideal form of the beloved object, then under this form is communicated to us this same unity-of-all essence. (pp. 89–90)

Marriage is a duality. In the world today there is a prevailing tendency to lead everything back, quite wrongly, to the sexual. A great antithesis plays into the realm of marriage: the husband has a female etheric body [of life forces], and the wife a male etheric body. The spirit and soul in the man is more feminine, and vice versa. The human soul strives toward the highest. Hence, the man will equate the highest with the womanly, because his soul is feminine. The external part, the body, is only the outer symbol, only a metaphor. "All things transient are but a parable." "The eternal womanly draws us to the heights."[26]

If women take men to the heights, do men take women to the depths?

In the Monastery of San Marco, I spent time in the cell reserved for Cosimo de' Medici. It is a special cell, and it feels awesome to stand where such a powerful man prayed or meditated. The paintings there are *Adoration of the Magi at the birth of Christ* and a small painting of the Christ with the crown of thorns. The cells are Spartan and one can truly feel the atmosphere of devotion once cultivated there in contrast to the opulence of the popes. Or as Dante puts it:

> The Gospel and the fathers of the Church
>   lie gathering dust, and Canon Law alone
>   is studied, as the margins testify.
> The pope and Cardinals heed of nothing else;
>   their thoughts do not go out to Nazareth
>   where Gabriel once opened wide his wings.
> But Vatican and every sacred place
>   in Rome which marked the burial-ground of saints
>   who fought in Peter's army to the death,
> Shall soon be free of this adultery.[27]

Perhaps Cosimo de' Medici was meditating on these words by Marsilio Ficino, whose Florentine Academy tried to revive Plato's school:

Surely the condition natural to our intellect is that it should inquire into the cause of each thing and, in turn, into the cause of the cause. For this reason the inquiry of the intellect never ceases until it finds that cause of which nothing is the cause but which itself is the cause of the causes. This cause is none other than the boundless God. Similarly, the desire of

---

26 Rudolf Steiner, *Founding a Science of the Spirit* (London: Rudolf Steiner Press, 1999), p. 143.
27 Dante, *The Divine Comedy, Paradise*, lines 133–142, p. 109.

Adoration of the Magi *(c. 1440), Fra Angelico and Benozzo Gozzoli (fresco in cell 39, San Marco Museum)*

the will is not satisfied by any good, as long as we believe that there is yet another beyond it. Therefore, the will is satisfied only by that one good beyond which there is no further good. What can this good be except the boundless God? As long as any truth or goodness is presented which has distinct gradations, no matter how many, you inquire after more by the intellect and desire further by the will. Nowhere can you rest except in boundless truth and goodness, nor find an end except in the infinite. Now, since each thing rests in its own especial origin, from which it is produced and where it is perfected, and since our soul is able to rest only in the infinite, it follows that which is infinite must alone be its especial origin. Indeed this should be properly called infinity itself and eternity itself rather than something eternal and infinite...undoubtedly this is the reason that there are none among men who live contentedly on Earth and are satisfied with merely temporal possessions.[28]

It is interesting that Ficino was no admirer of Fr. Girolamo Savonarola, and from their style of writing it is not surprising. One is a platonic, idealist thinker whose visions do not have much room, a more modern man or one who anticipated the modern mind. The other is a man of the church, living

---

28 Ernst Cassirer, *The Renaissance Philosophy of Man* (Chicago: University of Chicago Press, 1975), p. 201.

deeply with the images of the life of Christ—images that lived in his soul and left very little room for free will. Both were working toward the same goal, but in extremely different ways. One could say that Savonarola was a man living in the past, and Ficino in the future.

> What, then, are the distinguishing characteristics of Ficino's Platonic philosophy? According to this own statements, the choice of Platonism as source and framework for a philosophic system was determined by the harmony he believed to exist between it and the Christian faith. The use of Platonic concepts and arguments to support and develop religious beliefs was, of course, not an innovation, but rather a return to the tendency of the early Church Fathers. Ficino himself cites Augustine as his guide in judging Platonism to be superior to all other philosophies.... Ficino deliberately set out to combine the Platonic doctrine as a whole with the Christian doctrine, itself the result of centuries of incremental development. Such an attempt was possible only after the recovery of the complete and original text of the Platonic writers.... Ficino...regards the Platonic doctrine as an authority comparable to that of the divine law and contrasts it, like the latter, to independent philosophical reasoning. Not only is the Platonic tradition itself divinely inspired; its revival is necessary in order that the Christian religion may be confirmed and rendered sufficiently rational to satisfy the skeptical and atheistic minds of the age....
>
> The assertion that Platonism is of divine origin is related to the Humanistic belief in the universal ability of man to envision and attain the highest good. The truth and superiority of the Christian religion is not questioned in Ficino's writings, but this truth and superiority does not depend upon a unique revelation. Rather, Christianity could not be regarded as the true religion unless all men in all times had a desire for and a capacity to attain the same goal, the pursuit of which it defines as the only way to salvation. It could not be regarded as superior unless it perfected and facilitated the attainment of such a natural aim. Therefore, Ficino must find in the nature of man himself a basis for the identification of the highest good with the knowledge and enjoyment of God. The assertion that there is such a basis may then obtain support from the opinions of thinkers of other cultures and of other times.[29]

---

29 Ernst Cassirer, *The Renaissance Philosophy of Man*, pp. 187–188.

I am getting used to my own cell, a room in the basement of a large house, close to the wine cellar. At least it has one low window that looks into the garden at ground level. The ceiling is nice—not flat, but more like the cells in San Marco that have four arches meeting in the center. The room has a great and pleasant feeling as though it should have a fresco.

I buy more olives. At breakfast, lunch, and dinner, I must be eating at least half a pound a day, along with the local cheese, bread, and raviolis. What else do I need? It is Saturday in the city, the number of tourists undiminished. Many complain of how expensive everything is, making their own sandwiches and sitting on steps or walls to eat. The currency exchange rate is very high for most; a typical drink costs six to eight dollars. Continuing my walk, I cross Ponte Vecchio over the River Arno, and the famous bridge is mobbed.

Taking a bus, I see the little markets where people buy vegetables. Finally, I am able to see the local people. The old ladies do their shopping, and from the looks of the old people, Italians live longer and enjoy life. This morning, the owner of the house offered me a ride into town on his small motorbike, but I declined. Today, I am not used to so much traffic—thirty years ago, certainly. But now, I am too scared of the traffic, the bikes, motorbikes, cars, trucks, buses, pedestrians, cop cars. It's like a zoo. Beppe Severgnini had this to say of Italian drivers:

> In Italy rules are not obeyed as they are elsewhere. We think it's an insult to our intelligence to comply with a regulation. Obedience is boring. We want to think about it. We want to decide whether a particular law applies to our specific case. In that place, at that time.
>
> Do you see that red light? It looks the same as the other red light anywhere in the world, but it's an Italian invention. It's not an order, as you might naively think. Nor is it a warning, as a superficial glance might suggest. It's actually an opportunity to reflect, and that reflection is hardly ever silly. Pointless, perhaps, but not silly.
>
> When many Italians see a stoplight, their brain perceives no prohibition (Red! Stop! Do not Pass!). Instead, they see a stimulus. OK, then. What kind of red is it? A pedestrian red? But it is seven in the morning. There are no pedestrians about this early. That means it's a negotiable red; it's not a "not-quite-red." So we can go. Or is it a red at an intersection? What kind of intersection? You can see what's coming here, and

the road is clear. So it's not a red, it's an "almost red," a "relative red." What do we do? We think about it for a bit, then we go.

And what if it is a red at a dangerous intersection with traffic you can't see arriving at high speed? What kind of question is that? We stop of course, and wait for the green light. In Florence, where we'll be going, they have an expression: *rosso pieno* (full red). Rosso (red) is a bureaucratic formula, and *pieno* (full) is a personal comment.

Note that these decisions are not taken lightly. They are the outcome of a logical process that almost always turns out to be accurate. When the reasoning fails, it's time to call the ambulance.

This is the Italian take on rules of whatever kind, regarding road discipline, the law, taxes, or personal behavior. If it is opportunism, it is an opportunism born of pride, not selfishness. The sculptor Benvenuto Cellini considered himself "above the law" because he was an artist. Most Italians don't quite go that far, but we do grant ourselves the right to interpret it. We don't accept the idea that a ban is a ban, or that a red light is a red light. Our reaction is "Let's talk about it."[30]

I went to the Uffizi Palace and into the gardens. Later, I stopped for my ritual coffee (standing, because it is much cheaper), and then went to the market, which was closing. I found another place, where I ate delicious couscous with vegetables served by men from the Middle East. Africans and Arabs are right at home in this little restaurant.

I did not have to wait long for the bus back to Settignano. The weather has been great—sun and warmth replacing the rainy days that welcomed me when I arrived. I might take the bus and visit the seashore next week, and experience another city.

A beautiful Sunday morning, I begin with a run toward the top of the hills. Some nuns are leaving their little convent and going to church with the priest in the local chapel. Other runners are also enjoying the warm morning. The road meanders through olive groves, oak trees, tall ancient cypresses, and fig

---

30 Beppe Severgnini, *La Bella Figura*, pp. 9–10.

trees. The road is extremely narrow with well-kept stone walls and tall gates hiding fabulous villas.

When I return to the house, the owner is cooking something that smells delicious. I shower, changed clothes, and head for the hills again, this time on an eight-and-a-half-mile walk from Settignano to Fiesole. Again, a beautiful road goes up and down a forested mountain. Beautiful villas are hidden on large properties, and a medieval castle emerges from the top of hills covered with oaks and cypresses. I feel privileged to enjoy such scenery with no one else around. For breakfast, I help myself to lots of figs from large gardens, accompanied by bread, cheese, tomatoes, and water. I am eating like a peasant. As I take pictures, I savor the morning, walking gently from one hill to the next, with views of Florence on the distant horizon. The architecture fits the landscape and pleases the eyes. It all seems in proportion, comfortable and harmonious. To grow up in such a landscape must shape the psyche of those who live here. It's no wonder that Italians are the top designers in the world.

After less than two hours of walking, I arrive in Fiesole and, as usual, sit on a terrace to rest and look at the distant hills. There are many tourists who arrived by car are already enjoying their cups of cappuccino.

After a while, I head out to an old Etruscan tomb site. I try to put myself in the time period to understand how they transported such enormous stones. I can imagine them being pulled by bullocks on some sort of wheeled chariots tended by slaves with bare feet. Rudolf Steiner imagined it this way:

> Let us try to enter the soul mood of the ancient Europeans. They said to themselves, "I see indeed that I am connected with the gods. I reach upward into their realm." This led to the development of a strong consciousness of personality, specifically on the European landmass—consciousness of the divine worth of human personality and, above all, a strong sense of freedom. We must be mindful of this trait; it is this consciousness of personality that the Europeans carried with them as they moved south and populated the Greek and Italian peninsulas. In particular, in the ancient Etruscans we see late arrivals among those of this feeling. We can observe their strong feeling for freedom in their distinctive art, as they had safeguarded its spiritual basis. Before the rise of the Roman kingdom on the Italian peninsula, the Etruscans were there with a high degree of freedom in their form of government. Admittedly it was, in a sense, hierarchical, but in other ways it was free, even in the highest

One finds the arts, old and new, in even the smallest towns.
Here, musicians entertain on the streets.

A violinist busks on the street.

sense. Each town took great care of its own freedom, and the ancient Etruscans would have felt any kind of modern confederation intolerable.[31]

After meditating on the Etruscan site, I go into the town square, where I watch more people and a young girl from Norway serves me a cappuccino. After I buy some local cheese at a little market, I take a bus to Florence.

The city is full again as I head toward my favorite church. I sit in front to await a concert of sacred music with organ and a countertenor. I had never heard a man's voice sing so high. The singer, a handsome Italian, is dressed in black. He seemed to enter a meditative mood before singing variations of *Ave Maria* in his rich, high voice. As I listen to his magical voice accompanied by organ music, the church becomes alive. All the while, I am able to look at my favorite icon of the Madonna.

This icon is famous and is supposed to have miraculous powers. People come and pray to the sacred painting. The icon is the altarpiece in the tabernacle of Orsanmichele ("Kitchen Garden of St. Michael"). Titled *Madonna della Grazie,* it was painted by Bernardo Daddi (c. 1280–1348).

> In Daddi's panel, the composition of the scene, the Virgin enthroned surrounded by Angels, harks back to an archaic style, unusual in the Florentine art of the First decade of the fourteenth century: the host of angels arranged in steps is more reminiscent of the Maestà of Duccio [di Buoninsegna] and [Giovanni] Cimabue. In the painting, the theme of marriage, symbolized by the Child caressing the Virgin, is associated with that of the Passion, represented by the goldfinch in Jesus' hand, and both allude to the ideals of the confraternity based in the church. Even the choice of Bernardo Daddi, whose work was present in the city's main churches, denotes the desire to find a successful artist capable of painting an alterpiece that would come up to expectations: the devotional icon that the Captains of Orsanmichele wanted to offer the city. To get an idea of the extent to which the image was venerated, it is sufficient to consider that 1,238,400 candles were sold to be lit on the altar in 1359 alone.[32]

People at Orsanmichele guard the painting very tightly to ensure no one takes pictures of it. I tried and had no luck. The painting emanates a raw spiri-

---

31 Rudolf Steiner, *Universe, Earth, and Man,* p. 129.

32 Antonio Paolucci, *Sacred Florence: Art & Architecture* (New York, Barnes & Noble Books, 2006).

tual force that one can clearly feel. Watching others look at it, I see how eyes are drawn to this magical painting. Every time I am in the area of this little church, I stop and pay my regards to this powerful, sacred painting.

> Icons are primarily regarded as sacred images whose function was to establish contact between the supplicant and the saint depicted in the image. This immediate contact with the symbolized saint, who is personally present in his portrayal, confers a particularly intimate character upon icons. In prayer, the saint to whom these prayers are addressed as well as the icon itself become witnesses of human suffering and of the pleas addressed to the saint by the praying believer through the medium of the icon.
>
> This mediating function of the sacred portraits has led people to believe, since time immemorial, in icons being imbued with a special curative and invigorating power which found expression particularly in cases of illness. The curative power of icons is confirmed in a prayer recited during the consecration of icons, which refers to them as a source of healing and physician for all those approaching it in physical or emotional distress.
>
> Hence, icons were considered in particular situations as the proper remedy for cases of illness. Depending on the respective religious tradition, the cure would be effected by praying before the icon or laying the icon on the parts of the body affected by illness. In special cases, particles of paints were scraped from the surface of the icon and mixed with liquids which were then imbibed or rubbed into the affected body parts.
>
> In a similar fashion, particles of paint taken from portraits of saints in frescoes of Orthodox churches were used in the preparation of ointments and other remedies. When choosing icons to which particular curative powers were ascribed, the subject of the image was an important factor. For purposes of healing, believers preferred icons representing the patron saint of medical doctors or certain types of Mother of God. Prominent among the group of medical saints are St. Panteleimon and the brothers Cosmas and Damian. It is characteristic of all three saints that during their lifetimes they were active in the medical profession, thus performing quite a few miraculous cures, for which services they did not ask for any remuneration. This is why they are venerated under the Greek epithet of *anargyroi* ["non-mercenaries"] meaning *"those who despise money."* Also frequently deemed a medical saint was St. Luke, the Evangelist who according to oral tradition had been a doctor and painter by profession....

Icons and medicine as a topic have so far been largely ignored in art history and are perhaps likely to meet with greater interest in the future.[33]

I agree with the author, as my own work involves techniques for painting icons in watercolor.

At the end of the evening, in a thankful mood, I walk back to the bus stop for the number 10 to take me to Settignano. Tomorrow, I want to visit a monastery in the hills around Florence. I plan everyday to walk in the hills and visit the little towns. It is a good way to taste the countryside flavors. I love the old, gnarled olive trees, and next to them one often sees younger trees slowly taking their place. Sometimes an old tree is cut so that the younger tree can take over, or the two might intertwine with each other. Beautiful silver-green colors appear as the olives begin to turn black. I am reminded that Christianity was supposed to have spread only to the limit of where olive trees grow. I wonder what that means.

I fill myself with the ubiquitous olive and fig trees. Others take these sights for granted, but I immerse myself to feel the essence of those trees as I walk along the lovely hill roads. Mint grows among the olive groves, as well as marjoram and thyme and other wonderful culinary herbs. Olive trees seem to grow like weeds, though of course they are tended. Around the whole Mediterranean Sea, they range from Palestine and Israel to Spain, Italy, and parts of southern France, as well as Greece and north Africa. The Mediterranean seacoast means olive trees.

It is a rainy day in Florence; it cleans the streets and waters the gardens.

I have crossed Piazza de la Signoria many times, and it is always full of tourists. One of my favorite cafés is there with its great pastries. However, the ominous past of this piazza is haunting. It is the square where, on May 23, 1498, Girolamo Savonarola was hanged by chains from a cross and burned with two followers, Fra Silvestro and Fra Domenico da Pescia. A small plaque

---

33 Roland Burgard, Karin Nieswandt, and Peer Grohmann (eds.), *Ikonen-Museum der Stadt Frankfurt am Main* (Frankfurt, 1991), p. 298.

there commemorates the dreadful event. Here are some insights into this great personality from Rudolf Steiner:

> We have to distinguish the way it [Roman Catholicism] worked its way up to the thirteenth century—when it was, you might say, justified, because that was still the fourth post-Atlantean period [before the fifteenth century]—and what then followed, when it began to assume the character of a retarded impulse. It seeks to spread. But how? For it certainly spreads significantly. We see that the form of the state, which gradually matures in the new age, is more or less saturated with this Roman Catholicism. We see that the English state as it begins to grow at the beginning of the fifth post-Atlantean period is at first entirely in the hands of this Roman Catholicism. We see how France and the rest of Europe are entirely in the grip of this Roman element of hierarchy and belief system insofar as their ideas and culture are concerned. To characterize this impetus, we would have to say that there is an impulse on the part of Rome to permeate, to saturate the culture of Europe with this hierarchical ecclesiastical element, right up to the bulwark it has itself created in Eastern Europe....
>
> See how such things start. Everywhere, Romanism spreads in all shapes and forms, whereas in Italy itself, in Spain, the population is hollowed out. Just consider what an extraordinary Christianity lived in Italy when the Papacy was at the height of its glory. It was the Christianity against which the thunderous words of Savonarola were directed. In isolated individuals such as Savonarola, the Christ impulse was alive; but they felt impelled to grind official Christianity into the dust. A historical telling of what happened at the point from which Christianity radiated would have to say that the power of the Roman church element rayed out, but the Christian souls at the point from which this happened were hollowed out. This could be proved in detail. It is an important fact that something that radiates destroys its own inner core. This is how life goes. Human beings grow old and use up their forces. Similarly, cultural phenomena, when they spread out, use up their own being and hollow themselves out.[34]

In a passage by Savonarola, we will see that this famous man of the Church was anything but "hollowed out." His words were full of meaning and sub-

---

34 Rudolf Steiner, *The Karma of Untruthfulness: Secret Societies, the Media, and Preparations for the Great War*, vol. 2 (London: Rudolf Steiner Press, 2005). p. 115 (translation revised).

stance and not at all empty or hollow. The passage is taken from Savonarola's "Compendium of Revelations."

Passing the Church of San Lorenzo, one sees the outside markets with hoards of tourists and merchants from all over the world, from Africa, China, Japan, Brazil, the U.S., Canada, and Europe, all selling their goods. There are few Italians. Five hundred years ago, one could have gone into this church of San Lorenzo or the Basilica di Santa Maria del Fior nearby and heard Savonarola preach to the Florentines.

> For a long time by divine inspiration I have predicted many future events in various ways. But because I remember that Our Savior Jesus Christ said, "Do not give what is holy to dogs or cast pearls before swine, lest they trample them underfoot and the dogs turn and tear you," I have always been sparing in speech and not gone further than what seemed necessary to men's salvation. Therefore, my proposals were limited, although the exhortations, persuasions, and proofs I made were many. I never disclosed the manner and great number of the visions and many other revelations I had, because the Holy Spirit did not inspire me to, nor did I think it necessary for salvation. I did not think that men's minds were ready to accept them. Now necessity compels me to write down the coming events I publicly preached about, especially those that are most important and of greater weight. Many who tried to write these things down as I spoke from the pulpit have not expressed the full truth, but given one butchered and much mixed with error since the pen cannot keep up with the swiftness of the tongue. Some people, either through lack of understanding or wrong interpretation and malice, have spread my words among the crowd with additions, subtractions, and many distortions.
>
> Therefore I will try to gather whatever I have publicly preached up till now about the future into a brief compendium, leaving out the special manner in which each of the revelations was made and the scriptural proofs I used when I preached....
>
> Before I begin what I have to say, the character of prophetic revelation must be clarified in order to understand these matters. Each one can then understand how God teaches prophets the things they preach to the people. Because it is written in the ninth chapter of the first Book of Kings, "One who today is called a prophet was at one time called a seer," he is properly said to be a prophet who sees things that are beyond the natural knowledge of every creature, even though by means of the light

of prophecy he also sees many other things that are not beyond human knowledge. Since that light can attain divine things, it reaches human matters even more easily. Further contingent acts, especially those that depend on free choice, are far beyond the natural knowledge of any creature; neither man nor any other creature can know them in themselves. They are present to eternity alone because it embraces the whole of time.... Knowledge of future contingents is proper to divine wisdom before which everything that is past, present, and future stands open at the same moment, as it is written, "All things are naked and open to his eyes." Future contingents cannot be known by any natural light; God alone knows them in his eternal light. Those to whom he deigns to reveal them receive them from him alone....

Since the angels are in the middle between Gods and men, prophetic illuminations from God are presented through the angelic spirit who not only internally illumine and move the imagination to various apparitions but also speak to the prophets from within. Very frequently they even show themselves to the prophets externally in human form, predicting future events and teaching them the many things they must do. Through the light mentioned above the prophets clearly know that these are apparitions of angels and that the things the angels speak are true and come from divine wisdom. In these three ways, sometimes one and sometimes the other, I have grasped and known future events. In whichever way these matters came to me I have always grasped them as completely true and certain through that light's illumination.

As Almighty God saw the sins of Italy multiply, especially in her ecclesiastical and secular princes, he was unable to bear it any longer and decided to cleanse the Church with a great scourge.... Since Florence is located in the middle of Italy, like the heart in a man, God himself deigned to choose her to receive this proclamation so that from her it might be widely spread through the other parts of Italy.... Among his other servants he chose me, unworthy and unprofitable as I am, for this task, and saw to it that I came to Florence in 1489 at the command of my superiors....

Men believe that there is a great difference between knowing something by seeing it and knowing it from the account or writings of someone else. For example, if someone had seen Florence with his eyes and someone else had only an idea of it from the account and description of another, would you not judge that there would be considerable difference in their knowledge? This is especially true in the case of heavenly visions, where countless particular circumstances appear to the eye that are above man's power to write down or speak about. Although they are spiritual, they are represented to us through bodily appearances that are full of mysteries....

I grew weak at such an abundance of the sweetest harmony and awesome light. Again I fell on my face, but my angel strengthened me and lifted me up. I asked him what these wonders were and he answered. "These are the orders of the celestial hierarchies to whom God has given government of the world. The first hierarchy is closest to God and beholds the order of government in God himself. The second knows the same order in the causes and universal ideas; the third in particular things. And so the first order meditates the goal of the whole arrangement, the second sets out what is to be done, and the third carries it out."[35]

And, here, the tempter speaks to Savonarola:

The Tempter: "I think the fact that you have become a conversation piece for the Florentines and for the whole of Italy should be enough to keep you quiet." I answered: "My concern is to please God and not men, because as the apostle concern is to please God and not men, because as the apostle says, 'If I would please men any longer, I would not be a servant of Christ.' I am not so stupid that I do not know that anyone who preaches such things is held for a fool by the wise men of this world.... If you were only made a fool of, it would not count for much. But you are also hated and your life is in serious danger. It would be better if you considered stopping right now."

I answered: "As I said, I am not so insane that I do not know that everyone rebukes me and that every human state of life has grave hatreds raised against it. But the more I see my teaching, undertakings, and works to be like the teaching and works of Christ, the apostles, and the holy prophets who were mocked, hated, and persecuted because of the truth, the stronger I become. This is a sign of predestination.... This excuse could be admitted if you had exhorted the people of Florence to some good form of government, but you advised a form of government that seems dangerous to prudent and practical men. To put something of such importance at the discretion of the people and to snatch it form the hands of the powerful cannot be done without grave danger.

---

35 Savonarola, "The Compendium of Revelations," in Bernard McGinn (tr.), *Apocalyptic Spirituality: Treatises and Letters of Lactantius, Adso of Montier-en-Der, Joachim of Fiore, The spiritual Franciscans, Savonarola* (Mahwah, NJ: Paulist Press, 1979), pp. 192, 193, 195–196, 255, 257.

"If you look at this government correctly, it is right and natural for the people of Florence. All good government is divided by philosophers into three types. The first, when one person with full power rules the multitude, is the best if the ruler is just. The second is the administration of a few powerful and wise men, which is called aristocracy, that is, the rule of the best. The third is when a city or province is governed by the whole people; this is called polity. This belonged to the Florentines from old, and they call it a 'popular regime.' Ancient customs shows that one quarter of their magistrates, especially those who really govern the state, should come from the artisans. This government is not merely of the crowd, but of the whole people, that is, of all those who can hold office because they have been citizens for a fixed time. Because it is easy for the powerful to push the crowd where they want, we gave the city a style of government like a polity, or a popular one. If it is kept, after this no one powerful man will be able to gain a tyranny by reason of riches or connections. Only the virtuous will be exalted. The citizens will dwell in their city free of trouble, and no one will be permitted to oppress another unjustly. This type of government will give the greatest unity and peace. As I have often explained and as experience has taught, only three kinds of people will complain about it—the ambitious, the wicked, and the foolish. This is because, unless they improve, they will no longer be able easily to obtain the positions they unworthily desire." [36]

For words such, the vindinctive Signoria (a powerful man in Florence) arrested Savonarola and, with papal approbation, had him tortured. After repeated torments, he broke down and initially confessed that his prophecies had been self-serving lies. Soon, however, he regained his composure, renounced the confession extracted under duress, and maintained his innocence until his execution as a heretic and schismatic on May 23, 1498.

And finally, here is one of his visions:

Then that most holy old man Joseph joyfully grasped my right hand and brought us in when the gates had been shut. He said, "May your journey be a fortunate one. Rejoice, for you will receive pleasing new gifts, as you were told." We lifted up our eyes and saw a very broad field, covered with delicious flowers of Paradise. Live crystal streams flowed everywhere with a quiet murmur. A vast multitude of mild animals, like white sheep, ermines, rabbits, and harmless creatures of that sort, all whiter than snow, played pleasantly among the different flowers and green

---

36 Ibid., pp. 231, 237.

grass alongside the flowing waters. There were leafy trees of various kinds decorated with flowers and fruits, in whose branches a crowd of varicolored birds flying here and there in a wonderful way sang a sweet melody. In the middle I saw a high throne like the throne of Salomon....

On this throne there sat a most beautiful and gracious Lady holding in her lap an infant brighter than the Sun. Above them, almost in the middle between Heaven and Earth, shone a wonderful light with three faces that lighted up the whole world. The triple face seemed to take the greatest delight in the sight of that wonderful lady, and to fill her with light more than any other thing that could be seen.[37]

On my way to the bus, I went into the market stalls and bought scarves with beautiful designs and colors for friends and family. All the female tourists were buying similar things, so we all had scarves around our neck.

This morning I got up early and headed for the monastery of Certosa di Pavia. I took bus number 31, which was full of students, housewives, and old men. It left slowly through one of the old city gates and traveled across a countryside bustling with life, new construction, and gardens. The driver let me off the bus at the gate of a quiet private road that gradually took me up through a beautiful olive grove and Mediterranean herbs to the imposing monastery rising from the hilltop. It was fantastic sight, with little houses coming out of the rampart–fortress construction; these are the monastic cells. At the top, a few tourists were waiting and a gentle monk (probably a Cistercian from South America) took us around the beautifully preserved monastery. The monk told us that only a handful of monks live at the monastery, and that they lived only on what the tourists gave them.

Here, too, it seems unfortunate that these beautiful spaces are no longer alive and in use. These great sites deserve to be used again, with their beautiful, enclosed gardens, chapels, a large church, spacious dining rooms, and an olive grove. What a place for meditation retreats or artistic activities. The tour was quite short and allowed no time to sit and meditate. The monks' rooms

---

37 Ibid., pp. 247–248.

Certosa di Pavia from outside the cloister

had plenty of space and the view from their windows overlooked the whole area, but they were deserted, with only the wind blowing through the cold rooms. I would have liked to sit and meditate in those lonely rooms and try to capture some of what used to live there.

I headed back down along the pleasant road, the same way I arrived, and started toward the next town. I hitched a ride from a local woman who was shopping for her little bed and breakfast that she operates up the road from the monastery. She had been a school teacher and now enjoys meeting the foreigners who stay with her. Nonetheless, she complained about all the work. She dropped me off at the next town, and I jumped into a bus that went straight to the center of Florence, or Firenze as the Italians call this city of less than half a million.

I had another look at the Basilica di Santa Maria del Fiore, the *Duomo* of Florence, because I noticed that there was no line at the entrance. The space within is monumental. The cathedral, constructed from 1296 to 1436, is said to be one of the longest after St. Peter's in Rome and St. Paul's in London. The extensive use of marble gives it a certain coolness, while the geometrical floor

Named by Michaelangelo The Gates of Paradise, *the eastern bronze doors by Lorenzo Ghiberti adorn the Battistero di San Giovanni, one of the oldest buildings in Florence. Originally a Roman temple dedicated to Mars, it now has the stature of a small basilica.*

designs lend order to our chaotic world with its intricate inlaid marble work, which I could observe closely because it was not too busy.

I also enjoyed the stained-glass windows, which are glorious in their simplicity and brilliant, transparent colors. They are paintings colored by light, making it worthwhile to return at different times of the day to see them. Like others in this sacred space, I wandered, not really knowing where to look first; there is so much. The fresco of Dante, *La commedia illumina Firenze* ("The Comedy Illuminating Florence") by Domenico di Michelino caught my attention and reminded me of Dante's enormous influence there. When we read his *Divine Comedy,* we can feel his presence. After a while, I found myself going outside to see the Cathedral's imposing presence and to look more closely at Lorenzo Ghiberti's bronze sculptured doors of the Battistero di San Giovanni (Baptistery of St. John), which depict John the Baptist, Old Testament scenes, the Patriarch St. Joseph, the Virtues, and other scenes. I took many pictures of those bronze-relief sculpture "paintings." One of my favorites is the Marriage scene of Salomon and Queen Sheba, and the Ladies, the Virtues, *Temperantia, Justicia, Fortitude, Charitas, Prudentia, Humilitas,* and so on. I loved the different symbols for each of these women, as well as their solemnity and power. *The Gates of Paradise* panel is an exact replica of the original, which is in The Museum of Modern Art in New York. I often pass the bronzed doors and always admire them amid the other tourists, each time discovering new details and subjects.

Next I went to my favorite bookstore, mingling with the Florentines to see what they are reading, and had a cappuccino in the glassed terrace.

Another sunny day in Florence. I took another church-discovery walk and, instead of finding the one I was looking for, I discovered another not far from the Arno River and one of the most beautiful I'd seen. It is called church of Santa Trinita ("Holy Trinity"). It was constructed from 1258 to 1280 and has undergone major renovations that have lasted centuries.

Scene of Solomon's wedding on The Gates of Paradise, *east doors (top); Bronze scene, the baptism of Christ by John the Baptist, south doors by Andrea Pisano, Battistero di San Giovanni (bottom)*

The Virtues—hope, faith, charity, humility, fortitude, temperance, justice, and prudence—from the south doors of the Battistero di San Giovanni

Santa Trinita has many beautiful triptych icon paintings dedicated to the Annunciation. I took hundreds of pictures and planned to return. It is a bit austere, which allows the ancient icons to shine. The gold shines and reminds us of the power of the heart. I enjoyed just sitting and breathing deeply as I looked at the paintings. The painters, it seems, poured their love of the subject into their sacred work.

> True Love is always productive. For this reason, in this present time, as harsh as it sounds, it is almost only artists who have any sense of love while they devote themselves completely to a work they are creating. Thus the gods created our Earth, out of love as they devoted themselves completely to their creation and, so to speak, "sweated" creation out of themselves....
>
> Every enjoyment of art also strengthens the organs of clairvoyance. For example, when we look at a statue it is good to feel the forms and lines in thought. That strengthens the creative capacities.[38]

The morning sun shone through the little round window at the top, and a sunbeam was enlightening the space and some of the paintings. It was an unforgettable moment. Florence has thousands of such secret little places that one must discover, since they cannot be found in tourists agendas.

Last night I went back into the city to listen to another wonderful concert of *Ave Maria* and bought the CD. It was a moving two hours of listening to the rich tenor and organ in a little chapel not far from the *Duomo*. I do not know how I can go back to the quiet of the Midwest after this.

This morning I was going to do some writing, but decided I could not pass up a walk to discover more of the secrets of Florence. I visited Santa Trinita church again and admired the "golden paintings" as I call them. The fat brother/priest was there, running around and lending a distinctive mood to the church. It is good to see that someone actually worships and lives there. He resembles an old woman filled with intrigues. He may not appreciate my

---

38 Rudolf Steiner, lecture in Munich, June 14, 1908 (published privately).

taking hundreds of pictures, but I just can't help myself. Here there are dozens of masterpieces not confined to museums. They have their homes here and exude an atmosphere of quiet, deep, spiritual strength. There are also many students from abroad who study art and the ancient works of art in the church. Well-dressed Florentine women are here, as well, to answer questions. They are educated and donate time to help visitors understand their church.

I leave the church and walk up to Piazza Michelangelo in the Oltrarno area of the city to look for the church on the other side of Florence, across the river up toward the hills. I went into the wrong church—a long walk but a pleasant day. On my return, I wondered again through the tiny streets on the south side of Florence, which caused me to miss the church San Miniato al Monte (St. Minias on the Mountain). I went instead to San Salvatore al Monte, a much less impressive church. I'll try again tomorrow.

On the way back down, I venture into another area on the south, Piazza Santo Spirito, where I enjoy an outdoor lunch among the many other tourists. It's a local market day, including organic farmers selling their produce, as well as a biodynamic farm selling honey, cheese, vegetables, fruits, cakes, bread, books, and Rudolf Steiner. I feel like I'm back in New Hampshire at Trauger Groh's biodynamic community supported farm. Some farmers travel more than a hundred miles, from as far as Perugia, to sell their produce. A larger market that sells non-organic produce is on the other side of the Arno River. Here, however, are fewer people who wish to buy only untreated foods.

Later, I cross the Arno and walk around the *Duomo* plaza. For the second day, I see no line waiting to climb up to the church so I head up the five-hundred steps. It is expensive—€10 just to go up the stairs. At this rate, one could spend a hundred euros a day just visiting museums and churches in this city. Many cathedrals will remain unseen; my budget does not allow it. Instead, I discover lovely little churches and chapels without the mobs.

At the top of the *Duomo* is a spectacular view that looks down into the church. The marble floor has a large geometric pattern, and the very large round stained-glass windows along the circular walk are breathtaking. The whole top of the church is one giant work of art. One can see how the dome was built, with all kinds of pulleys and mechanical devices and bricks layered sideways in the arches to bear the weight in the little arch. It is a wonder to see the dome from the stairway—a marvel of architecture and engineering.

Santa Trinita of the Vallumbrosan Order of monks, founded in 1092; various paintings in the church

View of the Duomo from above

The dome is painted with an enormous fresco. How did they ever get up there? It's a shame that no one can really see it; they seem painted for the gods since there is no way to see anything from ground level. One needs an eagle's eyes.

From the circular walk on the top level, one can see, of course, but it can cause an aching neck and distort any photos because of the odd angle. In any case, I could not imagine a hell worse than what they painted. The ones who painted those scenes must have had very bad dreams indeed. There is two-and-a-half acres of frescoes. They must have read Dante's *Inferno* very closely.

> So I descended from first to second circle—
> which girdles a smaller space and greater pain,
> which spurs more lamentations. Minos the dreadful
>
> snarls at the gate. He examines each one's sin,
> judging and disposing as he curls his tail;
> that is, when an ill-begotten soul comes down
>
> he comes before him, and confesses all;
> Minos, great connoisseur of sin, discerns
> for every spirit its proper place in Hell.
>
> And wraps himself in his tail as many turns
> as levels down that shade will have to dwell.
> A crowd is always waiting: here each one learns
>
> his judgment and is assigned a place in hell.
> . . . .
> And now I can hear the notes of agony
>
> in sad crescendo beginning to reach my ear;
> now I am where the noise of lamentation
> comes at me in blasts of sorrow, I am where
>
> all light is mute, with a bellowing like the ocean
> turbulent in a storm of warring winds,
> the hurricane of Hell in perpetual motion
>
> sweeping the ravaged spirits as it rends,
> twists, and torments them. Driven as if to land,
> they reach the ruin: groaning, tears, laments
> . . . .

View of a Duomo from above

Florence from the top of the Duomo

> Three-headed Cerberus, monstrous and cruel,
>
> barks doglike at the souls immersed here, louder
> > for his triple throat. His eyes are red, his beard
> > grease-black, he has the belly of a meat-feeder.
>
> And talons on his hands: he claws the horde
> > of Spirits, he flays and quarters them in the rain.
> > The wretches, howling like dogs where they are mired
>
> and pelted, squirm about again and again,
> > turning to make each side a shield for the other.
> > Seeing us, Cerberus made his three mouths yawn
>
> to show the fangs—his reptile body aquiver
> > in all its members.[39]

Giorgio Vassari (1511–1574) had begun a cycle of paintings of the Last Judgment in 1572, but never finished it. Grand Duke Francesco I, however, wanted Frederico Zuccari to finish the project with the assistance of painters from the Accademia Fiorentina.[40]

> The Dome was unveiled in 1579: the Florentines greeted it with the critical spirit they have always displayed, and in the nineteenth century there was even talk of whitewashing it. The decision was taken to keep the decoration, although the question was raised again in the mid-1980s. The extraordinary restoration carried out from 1981 to 1994 has put an end to the debate.

Those climbing the 500 steps were not overjoyed by the spectacle. It was very quiet. Some hurried past, relieved to get up to where there was fresh air, others looked very intensely or laughed nervously. I was just stunned at the huge work of art that had been redone not long ago. I could not imagine working for thirteen years on what must have been a superhuman task, both in subject and in deed. Read Dante's *Inferno*. Of course, other subjects are painted there as well—the whole Bible—and they are heavenly, but where we were on the circular walk, the scenes of Hell are at eye level. Our noses are virtually in it.

---

39 Dante, *The Inferno of Dante: Bilingual Edition* (New York: Farrar, Straus, and Giroux, 1994), tr. Robert Pinsky, canto V, lines 1–13, 24–33, canto VI, lines 12–23.

40 Antonio Paolucci, *Sacred Florence: Art & Architecture* (New York: Barnes & Noble, 2006), p. 80.

A view of the Duomo dome interior

In the center of the dome is the painting of Christ, and below the Virgin, with various circles depicting scenes from the Bible, and the apostles looking from the center, everyone is there. The who is who of Christianity.

> Outside on top of the *Duomo,* the city and the surrounding hills looked like a painting and the famous red-colored roof tops making a beautifully arranged landscape. One could see the hill towns of Fiesole and Setignone, the river, and all the other domes and cathedrals... People were a lot happier with this panorama than the one depicted below! This city must be one of the wealthiest artistic cities in the world. The many tourists were delighted to be up there, flashing away with their cameras... bringing memories back home to Arkansa, Texas, Maine, Spain, Shanghai, Tokyo, Melbourne, etc.... Imagine a big star originating from that moment up top of the *Duomo* and then all these people flying to their destination across the Earth... like a star.... Of people carrying all these riches to all parts of the Earth... that is a wonderful imagination to counteract all the nonsense we read in the papers....

People come to this city to visit its museums, but there are few other places in Italy where what is the distinctive characteristic of our country, the only one that makes up really unique and the envy of the world, is so evident as here: the fact that the museum...emerges from its confines, occupies the squares and streets and spills over into the place of worship. The most beautiful Pontormo in the world is not in the Uffizi, but in the Capponi Chapel of Santa Felicita....

All this means that "sacred Florence" is outside the museums and inside the museums.[41]

At night I read passages from Pico della Mirandola, trying to live into that period of history. Nowadays, where is a statesman with such a philosopher at his side, one who spoke Greek, Latin, Arabic, Hebrew, and of course Italian? Considering the terrible relations among the Arabs, Jews, and Christians, we should read some of Mirandola's words.

> John Picus, Earl of Mirandola was born on the 24th of Feb. 1463. He is equally celebrated for his precocity, the extent of his learning, his prodigious memory, and his penetrating intellect. As the pupil of Jochanum, a Jew, he became early initiated in the kabbalistic interpretation of Scripture, and at the age of 24 years he published nine hundred propositions in logic, mathematics, physics, divinity, and Kabbalism, collected from Greek, Latin, Jewish, and Arabian writers.[42]

Perhaps in the future we will have a re-renaissance and we will kindle once again interest in what other religions have to offer and stop demonizing people because of their beliefs. In the words of Pico della Mirandola

> I contend that this enterprise of mine is in no way superfluous but necessary indeed [proposing debates regarding 900 questions about all branches of knowledge]; and if they will ponder with me the purpose of studying philosophy, they must even against their wills, admit that it is plainly needful. Those who have devoted themselves to any one of

---

41 Ibid., p. 39.
42 Arthur E. Waite, *Alchemists Through the Ages* (New York: Cosimo, 2007), p. 36.

the schools of philosophy, favoring for instance Thomas or Scotus, who are now most in fashion, are to be sure, quite capable of making trial of their particular doctrines in the discussion of but a few questions. I, on the other hand, have so prepared myself that, pledged to the doctrines of no man, I have ranged through all the masters of philosophy [he is twenty-four when he writes this], investigated all books, and come to know all schools. Therefore, since I had to speak of them all in order that, as champion of the beliefs of one, I might not seem fettered to it and appear to place less value on the rest, even while proposing a few theses concerning all the schools together. And let no man condemn me for coming as a friend whithersoever the tempest bear me. For it was a custom observed by all the ancients in studying every kind of writer to pass over none of the learned works they were able to read, and especially by Aristotle, who for this reason was called by Plato "reader." And surely it is part of a narrow mind to have confined itself within a single Porch or Academy. Nor can one rightly choose what suits one's self from all of them who has not first come to be familiar with them all. Consider, in addition, that there is in each school something distinctive that is not common to the others.

And now, to begin with the men of our faith, to whom philosophy came last: there is in John Scotus something lively and subtle; in Thomas, sound and consistent; in Aegidius, terse and exact; in Francis, acute and penetrating; in Albert, venerable, copious, and grand; in Henry, as it always seems to me, something sublime and to be revered. Among the Arabs there is Averroes something stable and unshaken; in Avecinna, divine and Platonic. Among the Greeks philosophy as a whole is certainly brilliant and above all chaste. With Simplicitus it is rich and abundant and [he goes on to list dozens of more thinkers]....

For this reason I have not been content to add to the tenets in common many teachings taken from the ancient theology of Hermes Trismegistus, many from the doctrines of the Chaldeans and of Pythagoras, and many from the occult mysteries of the Hebrews. I have proposed also as subjects for discussion several theses in natural philosophy and in divinity, discovered and studied by me. I have proposed, first of all, a harmony between Plato and Aristotle.[43]

One cannot be but lost for words when reading these works by Pico. What a monumental mind and such strength of spirit. I do not think we rightly understand the depth of this renaissance revolution and those who

---

43 Ernst Cassirer, ed., *The Renaissance Philosophy of Man*, p. 242.

were part of it. They had the monumental task of lifting our spirit to the gods, one large, sublime effort to bring us closer to the divine. They were preparing us for our own age, when we are plunged into darkness and the need for monumental strength to get up once again. Perhaps all of the hundreds of thousands of tourists who come here get a great lift and help to bring a bit of that golden sun-ray into their homes scattered around the world. The great spirits such as Pico della Mirandola and many others are still among us.

I finally went up to the church San Miniato al Monte, which I could not find the other day. The walk from the *Duomo* piazza is long but worth it. One crosses the Arno, followed by a walk along the river and up various roads and steps. One then follows a path with beautiful gardens and cypress trees and places to stop and look back or rest. Along the way was a young Japanese woman, an artist painting Florentine landscapes to sell to tourists.

San Miniato al Monte—what a beautiful church. Again I took hundreds of pictures and enjoyed this special space. It dominates the scenery and overlooks the whole of Florence from a large, high, circular terrace. Just below and to the left of the stairs is a large cemetery with angelic sculptures that look after the dead. Here, the dead are not forgotten but remain part of life. The final stairs leading up to San Miniato emphasize its simple lines. Above the main entrance is a large somber Christ and Madonna, and Saint Minias Mosaic.

> On the summit of the façade still stands the eagle clutching the *torsello* [a bale of twelve bolts of cloth] in its talons, symbol of the Arte di Calimala which had supervised the work on San Miniato since the twelfth century and continued to administer it until 1770....
>
> What predominates in this architecture is the taste for ornamental decoration in two colors that was very widespread in Tuscany. A scheme of Middle-Eastern origin [the use of polychrome in the area of Muslim influence was derived from Islamic art], it was very popular architec-

ture from the Middle Ages to the Renaissance, and even beyond.... The façade of San Miniato is one of its most significant examples.[44]

Again, the frescoes inside are some of the finest I have seen, as well as the large Mosaic dome, which is very impressive and dominates the whole space. It is larger than the one outside. The icon in the central tabernacle is spellbinding, like all real icons. Such delicate work, brilliant colors, and gold. Clearly, much love was poured into these icons. I spent a couple of hours bathing in the richness of those sacred works. The light streamed through the windows in the entrance and flooded the large space with a heavenly light, softly enlightening the large frescoes on the lateral walls. The colors are soft and blend into the meditative atmosphere of the church, which used to belong to the Benedictines before going to the Olivan Friars.

The frescoes of St. John the Evangelist, and Magdalene with a feather (a pen) is beautiful in its simplicity. It reminds me of the sacred writing in the Gnostic Gospel, *Pistis Sophia,* which sees Mary Magdalene as the wisest of them all. Here, the feather, or pen, symbolizes who this sacred woman was.

> It came to pass then, when Jesus had finished saying these words unto his disciples, that Mary, the fair in her discourse and the blessed one, came forward, fell at the feet of Jesus and said: "My Lord, suffer me that I speak before thee, and be not wroth with me, if oft I give thee trouble questioning thee.
>
> The savior full of compassion, answered and said unto Mary: "Speak the word which thou willest, and I will reveal it to thee in all openness."
>
> Mary answered and said unto Jesus: "My Lord, in what way will the souls have delayed themselves here outside and in what type will they be quickly purified?"
>
> And Jesus answered and said unto Mary: "Well said, Mary; thou questionest finely with thy excellent questions, and thou throwest light on all things with surety and precision. Now therefore, from now on will I hide nothing from you, but I will reveal unto you all things with surety and openness. Hearken then, Mary, and give ear, all ye disciples.[45]

The ceiling was also a very distinctive feature, allowing one to see the trusses that form the roof, giving it an aura of simplicity and nakedness. In

---

44 Antonio Paolucci, *Sacred Florence: Art & Architecture*, p. 80.
45 G. R. S. Mead (tr.), *Pistis Sophia* (Blauvelt, NY: Garber, 1984), pp. 26–27.

San Miniato al Monte (St. Minias on the Mountain)

Center: the mosaic of St. Miniato at the right of Christ holding a crown

the nineteenth century, they were retouched and painted with colorful designs. One can see the beautiful wood and wonder where it came from—perhaps one of the large chestnut trees that abound in the area. The church is almost nine-hundred years old. The large marble columns throughout the church are awe inspiring. One can only give thanks to all the stone workers who gave their lives to this work. This particular church took two-hundred years to build. The renovations are spectacular. It took hundreds of artists to discover the large frescoes and to make them come to light again through much loving work. Many were hidden behind coats of whitewash.

It is a celebration of Florentines and art students from all over the world, as well as tourists and their money, all of whom have helped to restore many of these ancient sights.

Yesterday afternoon, I headed back down into Firenze. This time I took a bus and got off at the *Duomo* piazza. I went up to the fifth floor of a large department store and to a restaurant on the roof that was packed with people. I spent the evening on the outside terrace, sipping coffee, admiring the city, and watching tourists. The *Duomo* was right in front of my face.

Today, I decided to visit the local synagogue, inaugurated in 1882, whose turquoise copper dome stands out among the many others. It took a while to find it, but I finally arrived, paid, and went through its reinforced doors. Once inside, I was stunned by its similarity to a mosque. I have always loved the beauty of Middle Eastern mosques, my favorite being in Esfahan, Iran, where I spent many hours in contemplation amid its stark, powerful lines, alone, peaceful, and open to the glorious blue sky with turquoise, yellow and white arabesques design.

This synagogue displays a distinctive Moorish influence in its Byzantine style. The decor is arabesque—not done as beautifully, although the feeling is similar. I find nothing of the human element here, no figurative works, but only elegant, intellectual arabesque. It is not an inviting, feminine space that warms the soul, but a more patriarchal, even fearful and foreboding, atmosphere. The beautiful woodwork nonetheless gives it some warmth against the power of the spirit. Perhaps one has to study Kabbalah and spend time with wise rabbis and the ancient writings to discover the warmth. I was not there during the service and the devotion of the participants, which bring in the human element of warmth. There are many candelabras for light, for enlightenment, and I could feel the great reverence and deep regard for the great, untouchable, almighty god. I think of these words from Kabbalah:

> We constantly aspire to raise the holy sparks. We know that the potent energy of the divine ideal—the splendor at the root of existence—has not yet been revealed and actualized in the world around us. Yet the entire momentum of being approaches that ideal.
>
> The ideal ripens within our spirit as we ascend. As we become aware of the ideal, absorbing it from the abundance beyond bounded existence, we revive and restore all the fragments that we gather from life—from every motion, every force, every dealing, every sensation, every substance, trivial or vital. The scattered light stammers in the intirety, mouthing solitary syllables that combine into a dynamic song of creation. Sprinkling then flowing, this light of life is suffused with holy energy.
>
> We raise these scattered sparks and arrange them into worlds, constructed within us, in our private and social lives. In proportion to the sparks we raise, our lives are enriched. Everything accords with how we act. The higher the aspiration, the greater the action; the deeper the insight, the higher the aspiration.[46]

After spending so much time with images of the Madonna with her loving face turned to the child, I missed them here in the synagogue. Nonetheless, one can feel the mighty presence of the spirit.

Pico della Mirandola mentions that in ancient times the great Law was not supposed to be written down but memorized and lived.[47] Could it be that the Law has lost its original power. Perhaps the fact that the Law has been written down is the reason so many young Jews seek in the East for the living teachings of Buddhism, abandoning their own tradition. In the following passage of some length, Pico describes his search into the great enigma of Hebrews

---

46 Daniel C. Matt (ed.), *The Essential Kabbalah: The Heart of Jewish Mysticism* (San Francisco: HarperSanFrancisco, 1995), p. 152.
47 Ernst Cassirer, *The Renaissance Philosophy of Man*, p. 249.

and Christians. But first, Christopher Bamford offers advice for reading great writers (Rudolf Steiner, but others as well):

> Every text is an occasion to encounter its author. This is especially true of spiritual writings. Reading the words of St. Francis or a Jacob Boehme, we feel we have entered the presence of and are face-to-face with a great soul, whose dedication and intimacy with the divine has allowed the spiritual world to communicate itself through it.[48]

Pico della Mirandola:

> I come now to the things I have elicited from the ancient mysteries of the Hebrews.... Lest perchance they should be deemed fabrications, trifles, or the tales of jugglers by those to whom they are unfamiliar, I wish all to understand what they are and of what sort, whence they come, and by what and by how illustrious authors supported, and how mysterious, how divine, and how necessary they are to the men of our faith for defending our religion against the grievous misrepresentations of the Hebrews. Not only the famous doctors of the Hebrews, but also from among men of our opinion Esdras, Hilary, and Origen write that Moses on the mount received from God not only the Law, which he left to posterity written down in five books, but also a true and more occult explanation of the Law. It was, moreover, commanded him of God by all means to proclaim the Law to the people but not to commit the interpretation of the Law to writing or to make it a matter of common knowledge. He himself should reveal it only to Iesu Nave, who in his turn should unveil it to the other high priests to come after him, under a strict obligation of silence... but to make public the occult mysteries, the secrets of the supreme Godhead hidden beneath the shell of the Law and under the clumsy show of words—what else were this than to give a holy thing to dogs and to cast pearls before swine. This custom the ancient philosophers most reverently observed, for Pythagoras wrote nothing except a few trifles, which he instructed on his deathbed to his daughter Dama. The Sphinxes carved on the temples of the Egyptians reminded them that mystic doctrines should be kept inviolable from the common herd by means of the knots of riddles. Plato, writing certain things to Dion concerning the highest substances, said: "It must be stated in riddles, lest the letter should fall by chance into the hands of others and what I am writing to you

---

[48] Rudolf Steiner, *Start Now!*, p. 44.

should be apprehended by others. Aristotle used to say that his books *Metaphysics,* in which he treated of thing divine, were both published and not published. What further? Origen asserts that Jesus Christ, the Teacher of life, made many revelations to his disciples, which they were unwilling to write down lest they should become commonplaces to the rabble. This is in the highest degree confirmed by Dionysius the Areopagite, who says that the occult mysteries were conveyed by the founders of our religion, from mind to mind, without writing, through the medium of speech.

In exactly the same way, when the true interpretation of the Law according to the command of God, divinely handed down to Moses, was revealed, it was called the *Cabala,* a word which is the same among the Hebrews as "reception" among ourselves; for this reason, of course, that one man from another, by a sort of hereditary right, received that doctrine not from written records but through a regular succession of revelations. But after the Hebrews were restored by Cyrus from the Babylonian captivity, and after the temple had been established anew under Zerubbabel, they brought their attention to the restoration of the Law. Esdras [Ezra], then the head of the church, after the book of Moses had been amended, when he plainly recognized that, because of the exiles, the massacres, the flights, and the captivity of the children of Israel, the custom instituted by their forefathers of transmitting the doctrines from mouth to mouth could not be preserved, and that it would come to pass that the mysteries of the heavenly teachings divinely bestowed on them would be lost, since the memory of them could not long endure without the aid of written records, decided that those elders then surviving should be called together and that each one should impart to the gathering whatever he possessed by personal recollection concerning the mysteries of the Law and that scribes should be employed to collect them into seventy volumes. That you may not have to rely on me alone in this matter, Fathers, hear Esdras himself speak thus: "And it came to pass, when the forty days were fulfilled, that the Most High spake unto me, saying. The first that thou hast written publish openly, and let the worthy and the unworthy read it: but keep the seventy last books, that thou mayest deliver to such as be wise among thy people: for in them is the spring of understanding, the fountain of wisdom, and the stream of knowledge. And I did so." And these are the words of Esdras to the letter. These are the books of the cabalistic lore. In these books principally resides, as Esdras with a clear voice justly declared, the spring of understanding, that is, the ineffable theology of supersubstantial deity; the fountain of wisdom, that is the exact metaphysics of the intellectual and angelic forms; and the stream of knowledge, that is, the most steadfast philosophy of natural things. Pope Sixtus the Fourth [1414–1484] who last preceded the pope under whom we are now fortunate to be living, Innocent the Eighth [1432–1492], took the greatest pains and interest in seeing that these books should be translated into the Latin tongue for a public service to our faith, and, when he died, three of them had been done into Latin. Among the Hebrews of the present day these books are cherished with such devotion that it is permitted no man to touch them unless he be forty years of age.

When I had purchased these books at no small cost to myself, when I had read them through with the greatest diligence and with unwearing toil, I saw in them (as God is my witness) not so much the Mosaic as the Christian religion. There is the mystery of the Trinity, there is the Incarnation of the Word, there the divinity of the Messiah; there I have read about original sin, its expiation through Christ, the heavenly Jerusalem, the fall of the devils, the orders of the angels, purgatory, and the punishment of hell, the same things we read daily in Paul and Dionysius, in Jerome and Augustine. But in those parts which concern philosophy you really seem to hear Pythagoras and Plato, whose principles are so closely related to the Christian faith that our Augustine gives immeasurable thanks to God that the books of the Platonists have come into his hands. Taken altogether, there is absolutely no controversy between ourselves and the Hebrews on any matter, with regard to which they cannot be refuted and gainsaid out of the cabalistic books, so that there will not be even a corner left in which they may hide themselves. I have as a most weighty witness of this fact that very learned man Antonius Chronicus who, when I was with him at a banquet, with his own ears heard Dactylus [a Jewish teacher of Pico] a Hebrew trained in the lore, with all his heart agree entirely to the Christian idea of the Trinity.[49]

We can see the length to which this great spirit went to find the common language in all religions. We will never really understand but merely take things literally as dead law and words unless we think beyond religious sectarianism, where the meaning of the holy scriptures is taken to higher levels, where brotherhood exists, and where a bridge crosses all religious denominations.

---

49 Giovanni Pico Della Mirandola "Oration on the Dignity of Man" in Ernst Cassirer (ed.), *The Renaissance Philosophy of Man*, pp. 253–256.

The Hebrew faith has seen many wise pundits, rabbis who have gone beyond religious sectarianism. Similarly, many Sufi orders go beyond the dogma of Islamic clerics. Catholic priests and nuns and other clergy, too, often have their own spiritual life apart from papal dictates. Such bridge-building is our work for the future. Pico was such a scholar that he could read the original sacred works and plunge deeply into their esoteric knowledge.

In the twenty-first century, sectarian approaches, whether Christian, Muslim, Jewish, Hindu, or whatever, no longer work. We have to get beyond them. Many of the religious are abandoning their inherited faiths to become Buddhist or to take up some other practice to replace the lack of feeling for the tradition of their upbringing. Everyone has different needs, and one must respect the choices of others. It is my understanding that we are born into a particular race and family not by chance but by choice: "This is what I need for this incarnation, this is what I need to believe and experience in this lifetime." If we view religious beliefs in this context, we can respect choices to become a rabbi, to live in an orthodox family, to practice Islam, or to reject religion altogether.

I left the synagogue and went to a little restaurant run by Jewish men. I was served a delightful Middle Eastern vegetarian meal. Fashionable young Jewish moms were also having lunch. I could have been in New York City. In fact, a young American Jew from NYC was cooking in the spartan kitchen. The little restaurant reminded me of the large Jewish quarter that was destroyed to make room for the Piazza della Repubblica. Building the large synagogue has been a sign of triumph over racism in this city. It makes a strong statement, on the Florentine skyline, which it dominates with the Christian domes throughout the city.

I wanted to celebrate the festival of light on Friday evening. I'd heard that the public was invited, but no one was there when I returned later on. One cannot be reminded often enough about the sacred, and in the old houses of worship such as this synagogue, the sacred is remembered for those of us who forget. I love to look at the sacred words. Something emanates from such written words that retains a certain power. Now, however, it seems we must find the sacred for ourselves and cannot expect someone else to do it for us. Priests, mullahs, rabbis, shamans, bishops, the pope, or gurus cannot do it anymore.

Many wish to become priests today, especially women. We are all called to perform our own sacred activities, and many people seek ways to sacralize daily life. Sometimes it is done in the way one prepares a meal or through gratitude in life, or how we garden or perform our jobs. We all want to put more meaning in everyday life, and no one can be satisfied with just one hour each week of church or temple service performed by a professional cleric. We want our lives to be sacred again, and many create their own little meditation space at home to retire for a few moments each day to focus on sacred words or thoughts. In this way the home can become one's church, temple, or mosque.

> Papal supremacy emanated from the south and reached its climax in the thirteenth century. In order to describe it in a way that is meaningful today and that fits the facts, we should have to say that this papal supremacy, which covered and dominated the whole of European culture, was essentially the ecclesiastical element of cultus and hierarchy, which was a transformation of ancient Rome into the Roman Catholicism that streamed into Europe, is one of the impulses that continue to work like retarded impulses throughout the whole fifth post-Atlantean period, but especially in its first third. You could, I might add, work out how long this is going to last. You know that one post-Atlantean period lasts approximately 2,160 years. One third of this is 720 years. So starting with the year 1415, this takes the main period to the year 2135. Therefore the last waves of hierarchical Romanism will last into the beginning of the third millennium....
>
> It is noteworthy that an impulse like this, if it is a retarded impulse, takes on an external character. It no longer has the strength to develop any inner intensity, but becomes external in character. It spreads out widely on the surface but has no strength to go into its own depths. So we see the strange phenomenon of Roman hierarchism spreading further and further afield, yet, in the countries at its core, being unable to give any inward strength, thus depriving its own population of inwardness.[50]

---

50 Rudolf Steiner, *The Karma of Untruthfulness*, vol. 2, pp. 114–115.

One can truly feel the hollowness of people today and the empty churches, synagogues, and so on. Sometimes, however, I love to go into the houses of worship of any denomination and partake in the sacred ceremonies of the past. I can transplant some of these sacred moments into my own life without judgment. Living in the moment, I enjoy the sacred moments, no matter where they come from. If I respect someone else's sacred moments, we can be brothers and sisters, especially if they return such respect for sacredness.

I recall several years ago standing on top of a mountain in Ecuador, not far from Otavalo, with a shaman Indian friend and my teenaged daughter. The shaman was performing a ritual there to give thanks for the sky, the mountain, the warm air, and the friends. As he performed his work as a keeper of the faith, I was deeply respectful of his sacred job. As the scented smoke from the burning sacred tree branch rose, two condors came and circled our little fire and then flew off. Then a little shower came and freshened our faces. It was a miraculous moment, a celebration performed by a respected elder in the Native Indian tradition of which I knew little. But we had a deep respect for each other's beliefs and shared conversations between brother and sister.

In his book *An Endless Trace: The Passionate Pursuit of Wisdom in the West,* Christopher Bamford writes:

> There is a new mood abroad. It is a kind of heart's need for a renewal of religion, a yearning for what religion should and once did provide, a seamless vessel of meaning within which to live, move, and have our being. Those who experience their lives as empty or meaningless are beginning to recognize that to oppose spirit to matter, locating all our problems in "materialism" does not work. Pursuing a "spiritual" path in a void leaves the world untouched. We need a context. The world and we are indivisibly one. Walking a path in isolation from the world ultimately leaves us untouched too. Thus, the realization dawns that "secularism"—the lack of the sacred—is a more useful description of our state than "materialism," because secularism gives us an ethical directive. It calls us to resacralize—consecrate—the world and our lives. "Everything that lives is holy," said Blake. When we seek Sophia, it is the presence of this renewing, sacramental vision that we seek.[51]

---

51 Great Barrington, MA: Lindisfarne Books, p. 16.

I return to the hills and stay home the next day to catch up on my writing and reading. As the morning ends, I climb the stairs from my basement cell for a coffee break. A stern, white-haired auntie is waiting for me at the top of the stairs, telling me to shut up and not to make any noise. I have no idea what she is trying to tell me, but she will not let me go in the kitchen to make a coffee. Then the owner comes out of his office to explain. He says there is a little baby in there, and that they'd had a hard time getting her to sleep and do not want her to wake up. He tells me that he will make a cup of coffee for me. So I go out into the garden and he brings a nice strong coffee. He is my age and divorced with two sons. The man explains that this is his little daughter. He had met a younger woman who believed he is a wonderful dad and wanted his baby. Now he has his two beautiful older sons and the baby girl. He tells me that it is difficult, however, because people think that he is the grandfather when he goes out with the little one.

My daughter arrived late last night and I walk to Fiesole again to meet her and her young Italian friend. It is a beautiful, fourteen-kilometer walk. I return to the fig tree and ask permission to take some from the gardener who was around. A jovial fellow, he helped me fill a container full of figs. I stuffed myself with delicious figs until I could not eat anymore—figs, olives, tomatoes, and bread are all you need here. My eyes never tire of looking at the hillsides filled with olive groves. In another month, they will ripen under the warm sunlight of fall. The sumptuous villas that dot the hillside are a delight to the eye. I am ready to move into one of them anytime.

I arrive in Fiesole and see my daughter and her friend in the piazza. We take a leisurely walk and buy delicious nut-sweets and local hard cheese from local farmers. Later we sit in the café and watch the afternoon go by before they take me home, where we meet the family. The former wife of the owner

Gathering figs and my daughter with her boyfriend

of the house is busy cooking a wonderful meal for her ex-husband and visiting her sons. They are having their Sunday meal together in the garden.

Once everyone had gone, we enjoy a chat. She is a lovely German woman who has been wounded by her divorce. I find myself in the middle of these social problems and cannot ignore it. Apparently, Italian men are quite barbaric. They throw the wife out, and the women are left on their own without a home. The home belongs to the whole family, so they cannot really sell it, so ex-wives have to leave the nest—the home in which they spent many years loving, caring, and building.

What can be done? Perhaps certain Muslims have the answer: keep the wife and add new ones—of course with the permission of the first wife. Such an arrangement does not seem as barbaric. They still care about the older wives, and they still have a part in the family. Moreover, the men have to provide all the wives equally with homes and wealth. My Persian sisters-in-law are modern and have absolutely no intention of including other wives in their lives. The West, on the other hand, has become barbaric in these cases. A younger wife arrives, fresher and more appetizing to the fifty-year-old husband, and the older woman is simply thrown out the door to fend for herself. Meanwhile, the younger woman finds it much easier to marry an established man than to make a life for herself. In Florence, I see many of these older men of fifty-five to sixty accompanied by young trophy wives. As the young women begin to age, however, the mess is likely to begin again.

I do not know how this can be changed; this business of relationships seems to be in chaos, and the married life of couples is becoming obsolete, much the way established religions and churches are going by the wayside. We need new forms, and here I see people trying out these new ways. Here is what Beppe Severgnini has to say on the matter:

> Many young people create an all-Italian melting pot, in apartments where a graduate from Milan lives with two students from Bari and a sales rep from Rome, who sublets to a construction worker from Brescia. These are places where spring-cleaning is put off until October, food is stored in the freezer, pasta with tuna is cooked in a dozen different ways, and a glass is raised for every celebration because it costs too much to go out for a drink.
>
> These are the frozen-food generation. There young people say they have 'decamped', an expression that reflects a healthy mental nomadism. Yet they have not turned their backs on their families. They know the power and the benefits of the eat-in-kitchen they grew up in. Witness the dirty laundry, guiltily handed over on arrival and lovingly returned on departure. The mums—the Tupperware generation?—cook ready meals. Just heat it up, they say with a professional smile. Dads helps with the rent. Grand-parents, uncles, and aunts contribute to the cell phone bill, provided they get a call every so often.
>
> If all goes well, a few years later these young Italians enter the next stage, of insecure jobs, a little discretionary cash, an exhausting social life, a first home, and heroic attempts to furnish it. Style? Just one: enforced minimalism with a Scandinavian touch. In this IKEA society; everyone has the same bookshelves, the same sofa, the same beds, and the same shower curtains. In fact, that's one reason why these young men and women feel right at home when they visit with one another. Sometimes they don't bother leaving.
>
> It's the new Italian family, and someone ought to study it.[52]

---

52 *La Bella Figura: A Field Guide to the Italian Mind*, p. 57.

Everything seems in turmoil, and people are trying to make the best of it, trying to have love in one's life, which is after all the reason we are here. Steiner tells us that Earth is the planet of Love. Perhaps more appropriate, "love in training"; we seem to be in diapers where love is concerned. We are at the prekindergarten stage, not advanced calculus, and have a very long journey ahead. Nonetheless, young people are showing creativity in their experiments. As for myself, my life has been rather unconventional and remains so. Not that this relationship business cannot be entertaining. In Boccaccio's well-known *Decameron,* the background is the Plague. Ten young people who wish to escape the plague rent a house on the outskirts of Florence, and to pass the time they tell one another entertaining stories. This one is called "The Tale of Filipa."

> Once upon a time, in the town of Prato, there used to be a law in force—as pernicious, indeed, as it was cruel, to the effect that any woman caught by her husband in the act of adultery with a lover, was to be burned alive, like any vulgar harlot who sold herself for money.
>
> While this stature prevailed, a beautiful lady called Filippa, a devout worshiper of Cupid, was surprised in her bedroom one night by her husband, Rinaldo de'Pugliesi, in the arms of Lazzarino de' Guazzagliotri, a high-born Adonis of a youth of that city, whom she loved as the apple of her eye.
>
> Burning with rage at the discovery, Rinaldo could scarcely forbear running upon them, and slaying them on the spot. Were it not for the misgivings he had for his own safety, if he gave vent to his wrath, he would have followed his impulse. However, he controlled his evil intent, but could not abandon his desire to demand of the town's stature, what it was unlawful for him to bring about—in other words, the death of his wife.
>
> As he had no lack of evidence to prove Filippa's guilt, he brought charges against her, early in the morning, at daybreak, and without further deliberation, had her summoned before the court.
>
> Now Filippa was a high-spirited woman, as all women are who truly love, and though many of her friends and relatives advised her against going, she resolved to appear before the magistrate, preferring courageous death, by confessing the truth, to a shameful life of exile, by a cowardly flight that would have proved her unworthy of the lover in whose arms she had lain that night.
>
> Accordingly, she presented herself before the provost, with a large following of men and women who urged her to deny the charges. She

asked him firmly and without moving a muscle what he desired of her. The provost, seeing her so beautiful, courteous and so brave—as her words demonstrated—felt a certain pity stirring in his heart at the thought that she might confess a crime for which he would be obliged to sentence her to death to save his honor. But then, seeing he could not avoid cross-questioning her on the charge proffered against her, he said:

"Madam, here as you see, is Rinaldo, your husband, who is suing you on the grounds of finding you in the act of adultery with another man, and who therefore demands that I sentence you to death for it, as the law, which is in force, requires. I cannot pass sentence if you do not confess your guilt with your own lips. Be careful of your answers, then, and tell me if what your husband charges you with is true."

Filippa, not at all daunted, replied in a very agreeable voice: "Your honor, it is true that Rinaldo is my husband, and that last night he found me in the arms of Lazzarino, where I had lain many another time, out of the great and true love I bear him. Far be it from me ever to deny it.

"As you are doubtless aware, laws should be equal for all, and should be made with the consent of those whom they effect. Such is not the case with this particular statute, which is stringent only with poor women, who after all, have in our power to give pleasure to many more people than men ever could. Moreover, when this law was drawn up, not a single woman gave her consent or was so much as invited to give it. For all these reasons, it surely deserves to be considered reprehensible. If you insist upon enforcing it, not at the risk of my body, but of your immortal soul, you are at liberty to do so: but before you proceed to pass judgment, I get you to grant me a small request. Simply ask my husband whether I have ever failed to yield myself to him entirely, whenever he chose, and as often as he pleased."

Without waiting for the magistrate to question him, Rinaldo immediately answered that there was no doubt Filippa had always granted him the joy of her body, at each and every request of his.

"That being the case, your honor," she went on, directly, "I'd like to ask him, since he has always had all he wanted of me and to his heart's content, what was I to do with all that was left over? Indeed, what am I to do with it? Throw it to the dogs? Isn't it far better to let it give enjoyment to some gentleman who loves me more than his life, than to let it go to waste or ruin?"

As it happened, the whole town had turned out to attend the sensational trial that involved a lady of such beauty and fame, and when the people heard her roguish question, they burst into a roar of laughter, shouting to a man that she was right and had spoken well.

That day, before court was adjourned, that harsh statute was modified at the magistrate's suggestion to hold only for such women as made cuckolds of their husbands for love of money.

As for Rinaldo, he went away crest-fallen at his mad venture, while Filippa returned home victorious, feeling in her joy that she had, in a sense, been delivered from the flames.⁵³

This week I have rested and spent time with my daughter and her friend—mostly shopping, since they do not like my "wanderings." She leaves soon, and I will go to Assisi for a couple of days.

We take a train to Lucca, a city of about 85,000 that includes a lovely old fortified town. The churches have ornate façades, but basically the same architecture. The lovely streets are full of locals and tourists, but here it is much less expensive than in Florence and fun to explore. We sit in the round piazza, which is quiet and hidden. It used to be a Roman amphitheater. Sitting there sipping coffee and watching people, time slips by and we enjoy each other's company. The sunshine warms us, body and soul. It's a lazy afternoon, indeed. Later, we take the train back to Firenze. The hills are dotted again with villas, farm houses, and castles, monasteries, and churches. The corn is growing, ready to be harvested for polenta, along with lots of nurseries growing trees and other decorative plants, and many vegetable gardens. The valley is one huge nursery. And of course the olive groves are everywhere. Goethe writes in his *Italian Journey*:

> The olive trees are curious plants; they closely resemble willows, losing their heartwood in the same way, and the bark splits. But in spite of that, they have a fairly solid appearance. One can see that the wood grows slowly and has an incredibly delicate organic structure. The leaf is willow-like, but with fewer leaves to the branch.⁵⁴

---

53 Gloria K. Fiero, *The Humanistic Tradition, Book 2: Medieval Europe And The World Beyond* (New York: McGraw-Hill, 2005), p. 11–12.

54 Robert R. Heitner (tr.), *Italian Journey* (Princeton, NJ: Princeton Univeresity Press, 1989.), p. 95.

San Michele In Foro a Roman Catholic basilica church in Lucca

I have become absorbed by the olive and fig trees. I have traveled quite a bit and always pay close attention to the cuisine of various areas and therefore also to what grows in the different regions. Today I was thinking about these wonderful olive and fig trees and others that are plentiful here. It occurred to me that, of course, the local people are very much influenced by them, as are the languages that grow in various ways in different regions. Here we have

Madonna sculpture on the right front corner of San Michele In Foro

figs, olives, all the wonderful herbs—rosemary, thyme, sage—the cypress trees, the yew tree that grows and resembles a cauliflower head, grapes, and, farther south, oranges, lemons, and so on.

The Italians have characteristics of the landscape, so what do they have that is like olives, grapes, and figs? Olives are soft and must be cured before they are edible. They have a peculiar, rich taste that is very original. It is a product mostly of the Sun. The Olive's job as it grows on the olive tree is to gather as much sunshine as possible on frequently dry hillsides. The sunlight is turned into a magical oil that is a heavenly gift to human beings. I would call it the milk of the southern country. Olive oil is extremely soothing to one's skin as it is for the internal organs. In Italy, everyone who arrives is soothed. I would attribute this to the soothing atmosphere of the olive groves.

Goethe came to Italy and his life was transformed. Tourists here feel different. Old couples hold hands, kiss, or are simply more affectionate. Beppe Severgnini describes Italy's social atmosphere this way:

> A town like Crema doesn't only look attractive to Italians fed up with traffic, and suburbia. Non-Italians like it too. You understand instinctively that it offers the right mix of unpredictability and reassurance. In the 1960s Luigi Barzini explained Italy's attractions for the rest of the world, and its peaceful invasion by tourists, like this: "The art of living, this disreputable art developed by the Italians to defeat regimentation, is now becoming an invaluable guide for survival for many people."
>
> This is still true, even though tourism has found many other destinations. Everyday life in a small Italian town is an ideal to which people more organized than we are aspire. We like our halfway Italy—not too big, and not too small—and have committed to it. A friendly store in our street makes up for bad news on the television. That's why Italy comes out ahead of countries like the United States, France, or Germany in quality-of-life-tables....
>
> Everybody in Italy feels important, and quite rightly demands attention. We know the pleasures of conversation, and savor the tang of personal observations. Comments on a new dress are welcome in Italy; elsewhere, they would arouse suspicion. Italian families defend mealtimes, and the younger generation is discovering the less crucial ritual of the aperitif. We've managed that most fleeting of habits: drinking an espresso while standing at the bar.[55]

A ripe fig tastes great; plump and slow to ripen, it is a bit chaotic inside, fleshy with little seeds and not very organized. Indeed figs are quite messy when very ripe, not at all like the internal order of an apple. Figs grow on a large beautiful tree, perfect for the shade. A certain sense of chaos in Italy allows one to get comfortable, but do not be deceived. The way Italians drive

---

55 Beppe Severgnini, *La Bella Figura*, pp. 175–176.

is highly organized amid all the chaos. Freedom requires chaos. There must be chaos before creativity can happen, otherwise nothing new can occur. Chaos, then creation. We all know this, but in Italy it is actually put into practice. This is one of the gifts of the Italians.

Italians resemble their language, of course, which sings and is full of vowels, indicating it is alive and filled with soul. Here, people cannot really be dead inside with such a language. Just speaking Italian wakes you up. If you feel depressed, sign up for Italian language lessons, or travel to Italy. It is cheaper than going to a psychologist and much healthier than drugs, which merely bury problems even deeper. You must live within the words when speaking Italian. And you must learn to use your hands.

> Abroad, they say there is no point in learning Italian. All you need to do is watch the hands. It's not true, but there is insight in the insult. Italian gestures are many and effective.
>
> Watch the hands of that squabbling couple over there.... Do you still not understand what those two are talking about? Let's see, now. He's got his fists clenched, so he's angry. She's holding her hands up, palms toward him, which means he should calm down. He's rubbing his thumb and forefinger together, which means "money." She is bringing the forefingers of both hands together, which means "they have an arrangement." So it's easy. They think someone's on the take. Still, I can't expect you to understand all this after just one lesson. You'd need a doctorate, but ten years in Italy would do instead.[56]

How can you say anything in Italian without being present. In English, it is very easy to say; let's say "How are you?" You may not realize you're saying it or even care. Italians seem to be fully in their spoken language. My grand-parents on my father's side were Italians who lived in France. The family compound had several houses, barns, rabbit cages, outhouses, orchards of cherry, plum, apple, and pear trees, vegetable gardens, strawberry patches, flowers. In Dijon, Burgundy, where I grew up until age six, I picked up the hand gestures of Italians. I also assimilated the arguments and heated discussions one gets into over making pastas on my grandmother's kitchen table. I cannot express myself unless I use my hands. Here in Italy, people constantly make eloquent gestures with their hands. It is part of Italy's attraction.

---

56 Ibid., pp. 69–70.

Enjoy speaking these words aloud. I think they will make you smile as you say them. (I used to teach Spanish, French, or English, depending on the country I was living in.)

> *e sanza cura aver d'alcun riposo,*
>
> *salimmo sù, el primo e io secondo,*
> *tanto ch'i' vidi de le cose belle*
> *che porta 'l ciel, per un pertugio tondo.*
>
> *E quindi uscimmo a riveder le stelle.*
> (final lines of Dante's Inferno)

It is more difficult to hide in this language, and perhaps that is why Italians are so able to read people. Many nuances cannot be hidden from Italians. I thoroughly enjoy watching the Italians, but the olive is still something to ponder.

Naples is a paradise, and everyone lives, as it were, in a state of intoxicated self-forgetfulness. It is the same with me. I hardly recognize myself. I feel like a completely different person. Yesterday I thought: "Either you used to be mad, or you are now."...

While Rome is conducive to study, here one just wants to live. The world and one's self are forgotten, and for me it is a curious feeling to associate only with pleasure-seeking people....

We strolled, in sunshine that was almost too warm, to the Villa Pamfili [in Rome], where there are very beautiful gardens, and we stayed until evening. A large level meadow bordered with live oaks and tall pines was entirely planted with oxeye daisies, all with their little faces turned to the sun.... It is most interesting to observe the workings of a vegetation that is never dormant and is uninterrupted by severe cold; there are no buds here, and only now do I begin to understand what a bud really is. The strawberry tree (*Arbutus unedo*) is blooming again now while its last fruits are ripening, and the orange tree also displays blossoms along with ripe and half-ripe fruits (yet the latter trees, if they do not stand between buildings, are now covered). The cypress, the most stately tree of all when quite old and well grown, gives me a great deal to think about. Very soon

I shall visit the botanical garden and hope to learn many things there. Nothing can compare with the new life a reflective individual receives from contemplating a new country. Although I am still the same person, I think I am changed to the very marrow of my bones.[57]

I will still ponder on the olive tree and see what comes to my imagination from it as a gift. I need to be still and let that great tree talk to me. I must *become* the olive tree through attentiveness and then perhaps I will discover more of its secrets. But such a task is easier said than done, as Georg Kühlewind writes (read this slowly, don't rush):

> What does attention consist of? Since it is neither intentionally directed upon something nor receptively adopting an idea into itself, it must consist of the same "substance" as the word or the idea: pure potential to configure. The attention can assimilate any constellation into itself. When one says: "the attention is directed upon something", it means that this "something" has been received into the attention. If it concerns the configuration of a phenomenon of the sense-perceptible world, the attention becomes identical with the *image* of the thing—the representational picture—and becomes *knowledge*. If it concerns the configuration of the *idea* of the respective object, the attention adopts the form (or constellation) of the idea. In this case the thing becomes transparent for the knower, transparent to his attention: permeable. This is the *understanding*, which constitutes *cognition*. What is formed in the idea or a word is subject to the human spirit—the "I" being in its unformed state—which is free and open to be configured: this is the human attention. Its substance is the same as that of the idea.[58]

Since the Middle Ages, the term *substance* has undergone an essential transformation downward, as happened to so many other words. In Scholasticism, and for Dante, too, *substance* stood for hierarchical beings: angels, archangels, cherubim, seraphim, and so on, i.e., understanding beings:

> Since first these Substances enjoyed the bliss
> of gazing on God's face, wherein are seen,
> all things, ne're have they turned their eyes from this.[59]

---

57 Goethe, *Italian Journey* (Robert R. Heitner, tr.), pp. 169-170, 119-120.
58 Georg Kühlewind, *Feeling Knowing: Collected Essays* (Fair Oaks, CA: Rudolf Steiner Press, 1995).
59 Dante, *The Divine Comedy: Paradise* (New York: Penguin, 1962), lines 76-78, p. 311.

Substance has come to mean the "being" or "essence" of a phenomenon. The word now has a meaning contrary that of the original; *substance* is the answer to "of what?"—exactly what is not the configuration, not understandable, not understanding. The English word *understand* corresponds directly to the Latin verb *substare,* of which the present tense participle is *substans*. In many languages, the word for "understanding" is a modification of the verb *standing,* as, for example, in the Greek word *epistasthai.*

> The intentional attention—directed toward something—is a preparation for understanding: this comes about at the moment when the grasping attention turns into receiving attention without diminishing its intensity and concentration in the process. Only what is conceptual, ideal, is understandable. But one should not conceive these expressions in too narrow a sense. We can speak about musical ideas, or ideas in painting, and the even higher ideas of the world of nature.
>
> Attention seems to be a bridge between the one who is attentive and the object of attention. Observing it more accurately, one notices that the "witness" who is attentive cannot be aware of him- or herself while intensely observing—in full surrender; if one would do this, attention would wander off from the object to oneself as another object. In both cases, the subject remains hidden and untraceable, because it is always where the attention is most intense. The subject becomes identical with the object of attention. The one who is attentive cannot be distinguished from that one's attention. (One cannot speak about an *attentive* one when one is not attentive.) The individual is given—to the extent of full identity—to the object of attention. The human "I" exists in its functioning, i.e., in its surrender; it has no static existence. It *is* only doing, in activity, in becoming—"becoming that." Properly speaking, one should not designate it by a noun, but rather by a verb. In this respect, it is participating in the way in which hierarchical being *exists,* who are also identical with their respective task, their doing. Therefore, the human "I" *is* in loving, creating, in surrender and attention. It consists of thinking, feeling, and willing attention. Self-encounter is possible only for "I"-like attention, for a self. It is known that only "I" being can recognize its own mirror image, whereas animals react—if they do—in a totally different manner. However, the human being normally mistakes its reflection—the sensation of the self—for the "I," confounding what is felt with the one who feels.

The human being as "I" being *is* wherever one's attention is. If it is with one's bodily sensation, the "I" is attached to it. In the New Testament, this attachment is called "the flesh." When this attachment becomes permanent, the autonomy, the freedom of attention, is lost, divided mainly between self-sensing and the world. The self-experience, is lost. Self-experience branches out into various more-or-less independent pieces of attention, which make up the psychological *subconscious*. But it is also dispersed among the countless learned concepts and representations. In the first place, schooling one's consciousness has the task of reestablishing the autonomy and undividedness of one's attention. In our time, this means schooling thinking, feeling, and willing attention.[60]

If you like to exercise *vos meninges* (your brain), as the French say, study Rudolf Steiner's philosophy of freedom.[61] I can guarantee a real workout.

It is a long road to the becoming one with, or the being of, the olive tree. The more one becomes concentrated—one-pointedness, as Buddhists call it—the more one becomes one with the object (in my case, the wonderful olive tree), the more you know the object because you have become it. "If we refrain from expressing our thoughts to things then the things will speak to us" (Rudolf Steiner, Berlin, Feb. 21, 1904).

Massimo Scaligero talks about this from another perspective in his small masterpiece, *The Light*:

> Philosophy has lost the human being. The art of the spirit cannot be the art of the philosophers, because thinking no longer participates in its super-individual source. In ancient times, however, the conceiving aspect of thinking could coincide with its self-reflectiveness where philosophers took on reflectivity as a vestment of thinking's power to penetrate the world's contents. For certain rare individuals among them, such a penetration was the communion with the world's essence.
>
> The *great enemy of the spirit is dialectical thinking*. Its infinite disguises includes spiritualistic forms.
>
> We must exhaust the world of words so that inner experience can arise. A sign of this transformation occurs when the practitioner begins

---

60 Georg Kühlewind, *Feeling Knowing: Collected Essays*, pp. 74–76 (translation revised). See also Kühlewind's *From Normal to Healthy: Paths to the Liberation of Consciousness* (Great Barrington, MA: Lindisfarne Books, 1988).

61 Rudolf Steiner, *Intuitive Thinking as a Spiritual Path: A Philosophy of Freedom* (Great Barrington, MA: Anthroposophic Press, 1994).

to feel nausea toward each argument or speculation that fails to respond to perceptions of the reality of the physical world or those of the spirit....

A meditant's strength is not enlivened by meditative results; that is only a temporary aim. It derives, instead, from the spirit by means of which such productive capacities can be drawn. Nonetheless, in order to reveal itself, such a meditative content requires something that can contain it and which is similarly free of any subjective content.

As long as we are bound to ephemeral contents, and as long as we can satisfy our souls with worldly or cultural interests—and that, let us be clear, does not mean that we must lose interest in the world or our capacity for human sentiments; just the opposite is true—and as long as dialectical thinking resonates into the depths where our capacity for representation is born, we cannot offer space within ourselves for the flow of the spirit.

In order to create space for the void (into which the spiritual world penetrates) to appear, we must master our capacity for representation—a capacity that we require for ordinary sensory experience. Normally, even if it is alive and rich, such a capacity is not truly *possessed*. We use it, but not with complete control.

The first task of the meditant is to experience that capacity, and to willfully experience representation, until one grasps its formative fabric.

In ordinary experience, we use representation to give meaning and value to things. These things comprise the typical contents of knowledge and, for this reason, they become important. Now, however, by grasping the experience of the representation, things cease to be content of knowledge and cease to be important other than by having a mere appearance of being necessary for our immediate existence. We train ourselves to take on representation as a content, and this becomes experience. By means of extraordinary willing, we train ourselves to devote unlimited attention to particular forms of representation.

By penetrating the representation, we can perceive the fundamental forces of nature in the form of images and are led to perceive the action of the spiritual world within the soul. By means of free imaginations and living ideas, we begin to see the spirit's language taking shape in the form of great symbols. We must extinguish this content if we want to feel the resonances of what those symbols help to reveal. The series of images, signs, lights, and colors is but one way for the spiritual world to announce itself....

The spirit flows into the world, but is ignored. It is ignored at the point where it becomes consciousness, because that of consciousness belongs to the sensory ream, as distinguished from that which *allows* it to become conscious.

The images in which the forms of nature and the world arise are the *imagining* that allows us to encounter the force that gives birth to them. This is its innermost force. We can experience this force before it becomes thought and before it falls into a form that is essentially opposed to its own light.

The logic of thinking—in contrast to the abstract logic of analytical debate—is the thinking that does not require isolated logical steps or a set of rules that inevitably lead to the production of each and every norm. Instead, it must have the ability to perceive its original dynamism in nature and in the world, that same dynamism that marks the presence of thinking in us. Our freedom lies in our ability to re-enkindle light in the form of creative imagination.[62]

All this in an attempt to understand how to experience an olive tree—what lives behind its *form,* its dynamism, or its *force* in Scaligero's term. The difficulty of understanding these passages by Scaligero reflects the difficult task of "being the tree." If it were too easy, we would be dangerous to ourselves. However, if I were to meet the kind of wise individual described by Rudolf Steiner in *Rosicrucianism and Modern Initiation* (January 6, 1924), I might discover the *olive tree.*

> I should like to give you a brief description of a man of the type one might have met from the fifteenth century onward, right through the sixteenth to eighteenth centuries. You might find such a man in a village, gathering herbs for an apothecary or engaged in some other simple calling. If you are a person who takes an interest in special forms and manifestations of the human being as revealed in one or another individual, then you may meet with such a person. At first you will find this man very reserved and purposely saying little, perhaps even turning your attention away from what you are really trying to discover in him by making small talk, so that you may think it is not worth speaking with him. If, however, you know better than to look merely at the substance of what a person says, if you know how to listen to the sound of the words, if you can hearken to the way the words come out of the person, then you will continue listening despite the discouragement. Moreover, if out of a

---

62 Massimo Scaligero, *The Light (La Luce): An Introduction to Creative Imagination* (Great Barrington, MA: Lindisfarne Books, 2001), pp. 96–97, 127–128, 140–141.

karmic connection this man receives the impression that it is worthwhile speaking with you, he will begin to do so—carefully and guardedly—and you will discover that he is a kind, wise old man. However, what he tells you is not earthly wisdom. Nor does it contain much of what we today call "spiritual science." He speaks warm words of the heart, far-reaching ethical teachings—not that there is anything sentimental about his way of speaking, but rather he expresses himself through proverbs and short, pithy sayings.

He might say something like this: "Let us go over to that fir tree. My soul can creep into its needles and cones, for my soul is everywhere. And when my soul goes into the cones and needles of the fir tree, it sees through them; my soul looks out through them into the deep distances of worlds beyond, and I become one with the whole world. Where is God? God is in every fir cone. If we do not recognize God in every fir cone, if we seek God elsewhere, we do not know the true God."

I want only to give you a kind of picture of how those men spoke—individuals that you might encounter as I described. Then he might continue speaking: "Yes, and when one creeps into the cones and needles of the fir tree, one finds how God rejoices over the human beings in the world. And when one descends deeply into one's own heart, into the abysses of the innermost of human nature, there, too, we find God. But then one learns to know how God is made sad through human sinfulness.

Those simple sages spoke in such words of wisdom.... What they gave, however, had an aftereffect of immense significance. You would come away not only with warmth in your soul, but also with a feeling of having received knowledge that lives within, knowledge that one cannot possibly discuss in intellectual concepts.[63]

From yet another perspective, Gerbert Grohman, an expert on plants, speaks of the olive tree:

> The Maquis Landscape:...the nights bring no relief. Drought sets in. Day after day, the Sun burns down from an eternally blue sky onto the dazzling white limestone rocks. Plant life subsides into "summer sleep." There are no more flowers.
>
> Only the plants which are biologically protected from drying up by their hard leaves or needles keep any foliage. So the color of the landscape remains green, even though everything around seems to have died

---

[63] Rudolf Steiner, *Rosicrucianism and Modern Initiation: Mystery Centers of the Middle Ages* (London: Rudolf Steiner Press, 1982), pp. 51–53 (trans. revised)

off. But this lack of activity is only apparent. Something is happening on a different level. The flooding light and the scorching heat inwardly transform the plants. Instead of outer appearance there is an inner activity. By the withdrawal of water no longer provided by the soil a new situation is created. Now is the time for the olive tree to make oil in its narrow silvery leaves, for the lemon and orange to develop their aroma. The fruit is being prepared. The bay leaf gives off a lovely scent when rubbed between two fingers. The sun-warmed leaf is more aromatic than the cold one, for the scent is stronger when the process is still active....

When open to the more intimate processes of nature one can experience the cosmic qualities which sink down into the plants. The oils and perfumes are materialized light, substantial heat. The plant is the living organ that collects these heavenly gifts. At noon the activity is most refined....

During the spring rains vegetative growth prevails and a mass of herbaceous plants grow and flower. During the following period of drought the process becomes more inward. It could be likened to an invisible second flowering stage which takes place in the green parts of the plants and gives rise to the oily and aromatic substances. Light and heat penetrate deeply into the plant metabolism. During the 'summer rest' vegetative life yields itself to the inflowing power of the cosmos—a thought tinged with reverence and awe. The ultimate receiver of the gifts is man. He harvests the oil and enjoys the delicious fruits and spicy herbs, whilst medicinal plants give him their healing power.[64]

I left very early Sunday morning to take a bus to Florence, and then a train to Assisi for a couple of days. I love riding trains; it gives me time to watch the morning grow as the Sun gets up, shines, and softly awakens the countryside.

We are in a valley, crossing from west to southeast. I notice several interesting cities, to which I return later this week, including Arezzo, about fifty miles southeast of Florence. We ride along the shore of a large lake, a remnant of volcanic activity ages ago. Continuing on, we enter the plain upon

---

64 Gerbert Grohmann, *The Plant: A Guide to Understanding Its Nature* (Junction City, OR: Biodynamic Farming and Gardening Association, 1989), pp. 108–109.

which Assisi is situated. The earth is richer here in Peruggia; one can see more farms, but there are still many olive groves, as well as pomegranate and other fruit trees, corn and soybeans, vegetable farms and nurseries, and the usual cypresses, though fewer yews. The chestnuts are ripe.

Goethe writes of coming down from Bologna into Florence and Perugia and into Assisi:

> I find the Apennines a remarkable part of the world. Upon the great plain of the Po basin, there follows a mountain range that rises from the depths, between two seas, to tend of the continent on the south. If it were not so steep, so high above sea level, and so strangely tortuous, it would have been affected more and longer in primeval times by the ebb and flood, which would have washed over it and formed larger expanses of flat land. Then it would be one of the most beautiful regions in this most splendid latitude, somewhat higher than the other land. In actual fact, however, it is a curious web of mountain ridges facing each other; often it is not possible to find the point toward which the water is trying to drain. If the valleys were filled in more and the flat surfaces smoother and better watered, the region could be compared to Bohemia, except that these mountains have an entirely different character. Still, one must not imagine a high wasteland, but a countryside mostly cultivated, even though mountainous. Chestnuts develop beautifully here, and the wheat is excellent, the crop already a pretty green. Evergreen oaks with small leaves stand by the roadside, but the churches and chapels are surrounded by slim cypresses.
>
> When I recently described what the Apennines *could* be, that is what Tuscany actually *is*. Owing to the much lower elevation, the primeval sea could perform its duty properly and heaped up a deep clay soil. It is bright yellow and easily tilled.... No field could be neater than this one, nowhere even a clod of earth, everything is as finely ground as if it were sifted. Wheat thrives very well here, apparently finding all the conditions appropriate to its nature....
>
> The hills around Florence are planted all over with olive trees and grapevines, the ground between them is used for grain. Near Arezzo and beyond it, the fields are left freer.[65]

Assisi dominates the large plain. Even from the train station it is an imposing site atop the mountain. In 1997, the people here suffered a large earth-

---

65 Goethe, *Italian Journey*, pp. 94–95.

The hills around Assisi

quake, and I was looking for some features on the landscape that would offer a hint of it. The volcano is not very far to the south, and I saw cone mountains of volcanic origin on the southwest side, as well as lakes that originated with volcanic activity. The area must have been alive with volcanic eruptions at one time in prehistory, and considering the earthquakes that occasionally shake the area it must still be lively today. The area is rich in Etruscan history and has many archeological sites, and many local cities are built on old sacred sites.

Etruscan culture lasted at least a thousand years. They were excellent sailors and were feared on the sea. They had a modern government by councils of twelve. The Roman empire destroyed that aspect of their small-village structure and replaced it with free civil life, after having acquired their lands and possessions, including the large villa estates worked by slave labor.

The rich olive oil and wine here made the area prosperous. During ancient times wine used to have a kind of liturgical use, somewhat like ritually smoking a pipe with Native Americans. Here people would share wine in a celebratory and ceremonial way, as may be seen from images on the vessels they used,

La Basilica di San Francesco, Assisi

which one sees in the Etruscan museums. Wine was a special, sacred drink and not intended for use by everyone. Perhaps we are all priests now—if we could only learn to behave in a more sacred way when intoxicated.

> There were ages in human history when wine was unknown. In the time of the Vedas, it was virtually unknown. In the ages when there was no drinking of alcohol, the idea of previous existences and of many lives was universal; no one doubted its truth. As soon as human beings began to drink wine, however, knowledge of reincarnation rapidly faded, eventually to disappear entirely from human consciousness. It existed only among the initiates, who took no alcohol. Alcohol has a peculiarly potent effect on the human organism, especially on the ether body, the seat of memory. Alcohol obscures the intimate depths of memory. "Wine induces forgetfulness," as the saying goes. The forgetfulness is not only superficial or momentary, but also deep and permanent, and there is a deadening of the power of memory in the ether body. That is why, little by little, people lost their instinctive knowledge of reincarnation when they began to drink wine.....

As the era of Christianity drew near, humankind was destined to enter an epoch of focusing on earthly efforts; people were to work toward the amelioration of earthly existence, the development of intellect and a logical, scientific understanding of nature. Knowledge of reincarnation, therefore, would be lost for two thousand years, and wine was the means to this end.[66]

The cultic importance of wine is alive and well in Italy; people, especially the tourists, are quite willing to forget themselves.

Lesson number one: people come here [to the bar] to drink, not to get drunk. Italians like being merry, but barfing on the sidewalk is not considered the high point of Saturday evening, as it often is north of the Alps....

To start with there is no legal age limit for drinking—or, if there is, no one seems aware of it. Families have the duty of educating children to drink, and for now the bottle is not an object of desire but a managed, pleasure-inducing habit.

Not all foreigners realize this. The Italian businessman who has a glass of wine with his lunch is frowned at by his American (or German, or Dutch, or Scandinavian) colleague, from behind a glass of mineral water. But at the end of the evening, the former will be helping the latter back to his hotel....

It is curious to note that we rarely boast about this self-control. We don't use endemic alcoholism of certain Northern European countries to humiliate them when they judge us....

The night is a legal drug, and free of the alcohol-driven inebriation it induces in other countries. We're not out to get wasted. We want to carry on piecing together our unpredictable mental architecture. The sky and the weather help. Italy's climate is an instigation to indulge. If we had Scottish weather in Italy, there would have been several revolutions. Instead, we lodged the occasional protest, made a lot of promises, and talked.[67]

---

66 Rudolf Steiner, *An Esoteric Cosmology*, pp. 33–34, 38–39.
67 Beppe Severgnini, *La Bella Figura*, pp. 39–40.

At the train station, hundreds of tourists pile into buses that drive slowly up the mountainside to Assisi. When we arrive, I climb to the top where an old fort had been built to defend the town. The view is beautiful; I can see far and wide. Walking inside the castle, I imagine the medieval soldiers keeping watch over this vast countryside. At the top of the towers, the wind blows from the east, and I can imagine that winter weather must be fierce up here.

As I walk around the city, I admire the marvelous architecture, the very narrow streets, and the recent renovations, which have made this city a real jewel. The stone walls seem to have been cleaned or rebuilt, while little gardens grow here and there, giving the feeling that, yes, this is a town where I would enjoy living. This seems to be a real community that takes good care of its city. The people are protected by the complicated little streets, so that sometimes you do not see anyone at all. The Roman amphitheater is a very imposing structure reminiscent of another time that is deeply silent now.

The Basilica of St. Francis flanked by large monasteries, is another bastion of the Catholic faith, an enormous compound, a whole city within a city bigger than the town itself, looking more like a castle than a monastery. Goethe describes it thus

> At Madonna del Angelo, I left my *vetturino,* who continued on his way to Foligno, while I climbed up to Assisi in a strong wind; for I longed to wander on foot through what seemed to me a very isolated world. To my left were the enormous substructures, over which, piled on top of each other in Babylonian fassion, are the churches where St. Frances rests.[68]

Goethe then stood in awe of the classical Temple of Minerva, also called Santa Maria sopra Minerva, which, architecturally, he called a "model building." We can understand Goethe's attraction to everything Greek, and why he hardly noticed the Christian church.

> The temples of Greece retain the basic principle of many Egyptian temples as dwelling places of the divine, spiritual presence. But the outer structure itself indicates a further stage. In the Greek temple's wonderful expression of dynamic power, not in the forms alone but in the inner forces weaving in the forms, it is whole and complete, intrinsically perfect—an infinitude in itself. The Greek god dwells within this temple....

---

68 Goethe, *Italian Journey,* pp. 96

The idea embodied in the Christian church is the temple as an expression of all that is most precious to human beings.... The Greek temple is self-sufficient, a single complete, dynamic whole...a temple dedicated to Pallas Athene, to Apollo or to Zeus needs no human being near it; it stands there in its own, self-contained, solitary majesty as the dwelling place of the gods.... The further people are from it, the truer it appears.... A Christian church is again quite different. Its forms call out to the hearts and minds of the faithful. Every detail in the space we enter tells us that it exists in order to receive the congregation with all their thoughts, aspirations, and feelings.[69]

The Basilica of Saint Frances of Assisi appears immense when seen with the large cloisters adjacent to it. A huge block, enormous, imposing buildings, not especially light-filled but a bit monstrous, which attracts many tourists. I spent many hours in the lower Basilica to be with my favorite murals by Giotto, Simone Martini, Lorenzetti, Cimabue, Capanna, and then remained for services, as I enjoy the singing of the monks sitting in the back.

The superior basilica is awesome as well, with the same painters, but difficult to view; with the head bent back, the neck starts to hurt after a while. Then one must just sit and absorb the whole place, which comes alive when the mass is celebrated. Otherwise it seems like just a museum as the sacred works lose their significance and value. The times when the paintings were made could not be more dissimilar to ours. People wish to penetrate their secrets but seem unable to. Here, one sees Germans, Italians, French, Spanish, North Americans, English, Dutch, Japanese, Chinese and so on. It is wonderfully powerful to see so many people travel far and wide to benefit from what was created 800 years ago. It is touching and perhaps indicates something positive for the future. I wanted to take pictures, but again it was forbidden, which was upsetting. I would have loved to take lots of close-ups of my favorite images. It made me angry; if no flash is used it does not harm the works of art. Visitors bring take their pictures to share with others, and if we multiply several images by the hundreds of thousands of visitors, perhaps millions of people would benefit. Nonetheless, the superior abbot or monk declined permission. Although one can visit their Internet site, which is very modern and hip, it is difficult to appreciate the real beauty of these

---

69 Rudolf Steiner, *Architecture as a Synthesis of the Arts*, pp. 5–7.

spectacular murals in that way.[70] The alternative is to buy the official book of the Cathedral (in 3 volumes), which costs €1,000.

The monks have no problem handling money. The basilica shop is in the lower church and sells books, cards, and many other items to the numerous tourists. Monks work there in their habits, handling money at the cash register, making it seem to me a mockery of what St. Francis taught. He wrote the rules for his order, which appear in a book I bought at their store: "The brothers are not to receive money.... The Lord bids us in the Gospel: take heed, beware of all malice and covetousness.... Keep yourselves from worries of this world and from the cares of this life."

According to the rule of St. Francis, the brothers, wherever they go, are not to handle or receive money or coins or have it received, whether for clothing or for books or as payment for any work, or indeed for any reason, except the manifest needs of the sick brothers. The brothers are not to think or imagine that there is greater value in coins and money than in stones. "The devil seeks to blind those who desire money or value it more than stones.... Let us then who have left all things take care lest for so little we lose the kingdom of heaven. And if in any place we should find coins, let us not have any more regard for them than for the dust we tread under our feet, for it is 'vanity of vanities, all is vanity'" (The Rule of the Franciscan Order, 8:6).

> And if it should have happened, which God forbid, that some brother is collecting or has money or coins, save only for the aforesaid needs of the sick, all the brothers are to consider him a false brother and an apostate and a thief and robber and as having a purse unless he truly repents. (8:7)

Or, as the Gospel said of Judas: "This he said, not that he cared for the poor; but because he was a thief, and had the bag, and bare what was put therein" (John 12:6). One can see how strict St. Francis was in his hundreds of rules for Franciscan brothers. Today, we live in a very different time, far indeed from that man of God. But to see the money handled in the church itself made the young monks seem like actors in the sort of play. They seem no longer to know the truth. I can understand why Goethe skipped the basilica and focused on Greek ruins.

Rudolf Steiner shared his insights into St. Francis:

---

70 The official site is at http://www.sanfrancescoassisi.org/.

One day, while Francis's father was on business in France—this again is a fact—a pilgrim came to Donna Pica's house, to the mother of Francis of Assisi, and said to her, "The child you are expecting must not be born in this house, where there is abundance; you must give birth to him in the stable, for he must lie upon straw and so follow after his Master!" This was actually said to the mother of Francis of Assisi; and it is not legend but truth that because the father was in France on business, the mother was able to carry this out, so that Francis of Assisi was actually born in a stable upon straw.[71]

After a dissipated youth, and a desire to become a soldier and join fighting expeditions he had a spiritual message, or dream....

> He heard something like a voice, which said, "Go no further, you have wrongly interpreted this important dream. Go back to Assisi and you will learn how to interpret it correctly." He obeyed these words, went back to Assisi, and there had something like an inner dialogue with a being who spoke to him spiritually and said, "Do not seek your knighthood in external service. You are destined to transform all the forces at your disposal into powers of soul, into weapons to be used by your soul. The weapons you saw in the palace [in a dream] signify the spiritual weapons of mercy, compassion and love. The shields signify the good sense you must exercise in order to withstand the trials of a life dedicated to mercy, compassion and love."... Thereafter he had a short but dangerous illness. He recovered from this and then passed through something like a retrospect of his whole life, which lasted for several days. The young knight who in his boldest dreams had only longed to become a hero in battle, was reforged, as it were, into a man who was now utterly dedicated to spreading the moral impulses of mercy, compassion, and love. All the forces that he had wanted to use in service of the physical world were transformed into inner moral impulses....
>
> Note carefully what took place there. In someone like Francis of Assisi there existed a tremendous fund of psychic energy, something which had existed as courage and fortitude in the ancient peoples of Europe, but which in him had been transformed and thereafter acted on the level of soul and spirit. Just as what worked as generosity and fortitude in ancient times had led to an expenditure of personal force, and had manifested in Francis of Assisi in his younger days as compulsive

---

71 Rudolf Steiner, *The Spiritual Foundation of Morality: Francis of Assisi and the Christ Impulse* (Hudson, NY: Anthroposophic Press, 1995), p. 15.

extravagance, so this now led him to become a prodigal of moral force. He was full to overflowing with moral force, and this passed over to those to whom he turned his love.

You must realize that this moral force is a reality, just as much a reality as the air we breathe, without which we could not live. It is a reality which flooded the whole being of Francis of Assisi and from there streamed into every heart he turned to, for Francis of Assisi was prodigal of a wealth of forces. This reality is something that has streamed into and mingled with the whole mature life of Europe; it is something that has been transformed into a force of soul and worked in this way into the outer world....

Some centuries into the Christian era, a kind of occult school was founded on the shores of the Black Sea [ca. 700–800]. This school was led by people who had as their highest ideal the part of the Buddha's teaching that we have characterized. But the teachers in this school could illuminate the Buddha's teaching with a new light, as it were, because they had also absorbed the Christian impulse....

The pupils in this occult school were divided into two groups, according to their degree of maturity. This refers to those pupils who had already gone through the preparatory stage, so that most of them could clairvoyantly experience a being who strove with all its might to bring its impulses through to the physical world, even though it did not itself descend to the physical plane. They thus experienced all the secrets of the Buddha and all that he wished to accomplish. Most of these pupils remained clairvoyants as such, but there were some who not only had knowledge and psychic clairvoyance, but also developed a spiritual element, which cannot be separated from a certain humility, a certain highly evolved capacity for devotion. These were able then, precisely in this occult school, to receive the Christ impulse to a tremendous degree.... Thus two groups went out from this school, one that had the impulse to spread the teachings of the Buddha—though they did not use his name—and a second one that also received the Christ impulse.

Now the difference between these two groups did not appear so strongly in that particular incarnation, but only in the next. The pupils who had come as far as the Buddha impulse, but who had not receive the Christ impulse, became the teachers of human equality and brotherhood. On the other hand, the pupils who had received the Christ impulse, were such that in their next physical incarnation the Christ impulse worked on further, so that they not only could teach (though they did not regard this as their chief task), but could work more especially through their moral power. One such pupil of occult school on the Black Sea was born in his next incarnation as Francis of Assisi. It is not surprising, then, that there lived in him the wisdom he had received about brotherhood and human equality, about the need to love all human beings equally, and that his soul was permeated and strengthened by the Christ impulse.

How did this Christ impulse work on further in Francis of Assisi? It acted in such a way that, when he was placed in a population in which the old demons of disease were especially active, the Christ impulse approached the disease demons through him and absorbed their evil substance into itself, thereby removing it from the people. Earlier the Christ impulse had embodied itself in this substance in such a way that it appeared to Francis of Assisi as a vision—as the vision in which he saw the palace and was called to take up the burden of poverty. This was the point at which the Christ impulse again became alive in him, and it then streamed out from him and laid hold of the disease demons. His moral forces became so strong thereby that they could remove the harmful spiritual substance [which grows on fear] that accompanied the disease we have mentioned [leprosy]. Only in this manner was it possible to bring to higher development what I have described as the aftereffect of the old Atlantean element, to sweep the evil substances away from the Earth and purify the European world.[72]

Read the whole book for a more complete picture. The mystery center in the Transcaucasia region on the Black Sea was that of the Colchis, made famous in legends of the Golden Fleece.[73]

Here is a story about St. Francis that portrays his moral strength and what he was up against:

> When he [Francis] had to discuss the final text of his rule with [Cardinal] Ugolino in Rome he felt he must accept the cardinal's invitation to stay in his palace.... The ministers, his Vicar and his Cardinal Protector were unanimous in believing the discipline of the gospels was too radical for the thousands of men—especially the priests—now joining the order.
>
> Unwilling to argue with the prelate to whom he owed personal obedience Francis attempted to make his point, as always, by example. Before dinner one day he went out discreetly to beg for some food. When

---

72 Ibid., pp. 18–19, 21, 33
73 See Lona Truding, *A Miracle for Our Time: Studies in Esoteric Christianity* (London: Temple Lodge, 1994), chapter 2, "Mysteries of the Black Sea."

he returned he found that Ugolino and his guests—nobles, knights, and chaplains—were already seated. He therefore took his usual place beside the cardinal and after the meal had begun handed out some of his alms to the company around the table, who received them with courtesy. Some ate the crusts while others kept them as mementos of this strange little interlude.

Upset, but too proud to say anything in front of his guests, the cardinal afterward drew Francis into the next room, asking with a smile, "Why, my simple brother, did you shame me by going out begging from my house?"

"On the contrary, my Lord, "Francis replied, "when a servant performs his duty obediently he does great honor to his master. I have to be a model for those poor friars, especially as I know there are some who are too proud to demean themselves by begging or carrying out any other servile tasks.

"I particularly don't want to be ashamed of begging when I am staying with you or other men amply endowed with worldly goods, for I must remember that God came down rich and glorious in his majesty to live with us who are poor and despised by humanity. I want the friars to know that I find greater consolation in sharing their wretched food than in sitting at your lavish table, for the bread of charity is holy."[74]

Dante, too, writes beautifully about St. Francis:

> Now I shall speak of only one, for praise
> of one, no matter which, is praise of both,
> for both their labors served a single end.
> Between the Topine and the stream that flows
> down from that hill the blest Ubaldo chose,
> a fertile slope hangs from a lofty mountain
> which sends Perugia gusts of cold and heat
> through Porta Sole, and behind it Gualdo
> grieves with Nocera for their heavy yoke.
> Born on this slope where steepness breaks the most,
> a Sun rose to the world as radiantly

---

[74] Adrian House, *Francis of Assisi: A Revolutionary Life* (Mahwah, NJ: HiddenSpring, 2001) pp. 243-244.

as this Sun here does sometimes from the Ganges;

thus, when this town is named let none call it
    Ascesi, for the word would not suffice—
    much more precise a word is *Orient*.

Only a few years after he had risen
    did his invigorating powers begin
    to penetrate the Earth with a new strength:

while still a youth he braved his father's wrath,
    because he loved a lady to whom all [lady *poverty*]
    would bar their door as if to death itself.

Before the bishop's court *et coram patre*
    he took this lady as his lawful wife;
    from day to day he loved her more and more.

Bereft of her first spouse, despised, ignored
    she waited eleven hundred years and more,
    living without a lover till he came

    . . . .

Enough of such allusions. In plain words
    take Francis, now, and Poverty to be
    the lovers in the story I have told.

Their sweet accord, their faces spread with bliss,
    the love, the mystery, their tender looks
    gave rise in others' hearts to holy thoughts;

    . . . .

The souls who followed him in poverty
    grew more and more, and then this archimandrite—
    whose wonder-working life were better sung

By Heaven's highest angels—saw his work
    crowned once again, now by Honorius
    through inspiration of the Holy Spirit.

Then in the haughty presence of the Sultan,
    urged bay a burning thirst for martyrdom,
    he preached Christ and his blessèd followers,

> but finding no one ripe for harvest there,
>> and loath to waste his labors, he returned
>> to reap a crop in the Italian fields;
>
> then on the bare rock between Arno and Tiber
>> he took upon himself Christ's holy wounds,
>> and for two years he wore this final seal.
>
> When it pleased Him who had ordained that soul
>> for such great good to call him to Himself,
>> rewarding him on high for lowliness,
>
> he and his brothers, as to rightful heirs,
>> commanded his most deeply cherished lady,
>> commanding them to love her faithfully;
>
> and in the lap of poverty he chose
>> to die, wanting no other bier—from there
>> that pristine soul returned to its own realm.[75]

I was sitting at a café in the Piazza del Comune near the Temple of Minerve and saw a young man who had long hair, a beard, a real robe, though not the very expensive kind that looks as if designed by Yves Saint Laurent (we are in Italy, after all), and wore sandals and socks. He was in his twenties and looked like a real monk, but he did not seem to belong with the other black-robed men I saw wandering around. The sisters looked to me more truthful than the brothers for some reasons. In the church, the sisters were the ones doing all the chores—changing linens, bringing flowers, and generally caring for the monks from smaller monasteries. I saw many of them driving cars and they looked very well-off. But I saw no monks driving cars. It is an intriguing world. Many of the priests I have observed in the churches (when they are around, which is rarely) look like bitchy, fussy old ladies—though that only endeared them to me. They had removed half the human race from their lives, and many of them

---

75 Dante, *The Divine Comedy, Volume 3: Paradise* (tr. Mark Musa), canto XI lines 40–66, 73–78, 94–117, pp. 134–136,

have become somewhat womanly in their old age. I would say the same for the woman's side, which bans men; in their old age, they seem to become manly.

Human nature does not like to be fooled, it seems. Men and women are made to complement each other, and when this is ignored, the body will compensate for the lacking gender balance—an interesting thought. But of course there are exceptions. My old friend, an Irish Dominican nun, is as womanly, wise, learned, scholarly, and joyful as a nun would ever want to be. She is eighty-six and still going strong, a true woman of faith, questioning and learning until the day she leaves this world. Her book *Earth-Friendly: Re-Visioning Science and Spirituality through Aristotle, Thomas Aquinas, and Rudolf Steiner* (Lindisfarne Books, 2004) is wonderfully insightful. My friend Sister Adrian Hofstetter shared a story with me about the nuns in her ashram or monastery. She said that the priests saying mass at her place were complaining that the nuns no longer came to the services or Mass. The reason was that the nuns were practicing Buddhist meditation in their rooms and had no need to celebrate the Mass. I thought that her wonderful story reflected the spiritual revolution in the world today. The nuns are not at all outside of it, but right in the midst of religion and devotion.

My friend is on top of this. She has studied everything one can imagine—from ancient mysteries to African, Indian and South American shamanism, as well as Buddhist and Chinese masters, all in addition to being a Catholic nun. She attends seminars on transformation, theater, singing, and farming and was a professor of chemistry for many years. I'd always thought that nuns were stuck in their convents. They are living the true Christian life and helping others in their communities.

Steiner gave an enlightening lecture cycle *The Temple Legend*. Perhaps these few passages will entice the reader to read the whole book. While reading, it may help to have a pen and paper to illustrate these words by doing whatever comes to mind. Steiner's lecture of that morning had been given to men only, while this one was given to an audience of only women.

> The whole fertilizing and fructifying force by which a new person is created used to be combined in one sex. Then the human being was separated into male and female. Which sex can best lay claim to the generative power? It is the female. Therefore, Zeus, who was worshipped as the progenitor of the human race, was portrayed in the oldest versions

of Greek mythology as having female breasts. Zeus, as a superhuman being, was closer to the female gender. The female was thus the first, or earliest, and at the time contained the power to reproduce a complete human individual. Such generative power was within a human being of undivided sex, who tended, in physical form, more toward the female. In this single-sexed human being, the fertilizing principle was wisdom, the spirit itself....

Now you understand what it was through which a woman could give birth to a human being. Physically, there is first a woman fertilized from above. It was the Divine Spirit in the woman that was the fertilizing principle. With the separation of the sexes, differentiation began in the transformation of the female spiritual organs of wisdom. The masculine power that the woman had within herself transformed that creative force into organs of wisdom. Thus half of the generative force stayed with the woman, and the creative physical forces stayed with the man. As a result of this separation, the spinal cord and the brain with nerve branches appeared, as portrayed in the Tree of Life and the Tree of knowledge....

Now the new beings adapt to the change. The individuals who had previously been female did not all take on the female form. The female side—the capacity to reproduce human beings—withdrew from one section and left behind, in substitution, the power to fertilize in quite a different way. Physical nature had divided itself into what fertilized and what needed to be fertilized. Spiritual nature, too, had similarly divided itself. In female individuals, the spirit acquired male character and colorings; in the male the spirit had a female character. This is still the female within the man....

What happened as the result of the female separating from the male? Which of the sexes still possessed a shadow of that power of productive spiritual wisdom—the male or the female? We have seen that the wisdom of the female actually had a male character; this is the creative, the productive, the intuitive, what is original, what is fertile. The same divine power that previously worked within a woman to fertilize and to reproduce the physical human being now worked as fertilizing principle in the perception of the divine center in the man's being. Religions work through words and images to further this process.

The female being becomes physically infertile, in the sense that she cannot produce offsprings out of herself as she did before. The masculine, passive spirit is the one that is spiritually infertile, but the man is the one who can fertilize physically. Spiritually, he now lets himself be fertilized by everything in the world; he becomes spiritually fertilized so that he himself can fertilize physically. The whole world penetrates him first; he becomes fertilized spiritually, the woman physically. Woman, by contrast, is spiritually self-fertilizing, whereas a man is fertilized by the spirit. The male wisdom is fertilized by everything external being gathered and combined. Male wisdom thus resulted that was orientated toward assembling worldly wisdom. Initially, this kind of wisdom was not actually present as what flowed from above; first it had to be put together by perceiving the physical world. Female wisdom, by contrast, was actually transferred to the priesthood. The wisdom of the priest turns out to be a property derived originally from the ancient feminine wisdom. Indeed, only if he was separated into two sexes could Jehovah maintain the human race. Two opposing factions resulted: Freemasonry and priestly rule, which were symbolized by Cain and Abel.

A difference exists between female priestly wisdom and male aspiration. This is described for us in the legend of Cain and Abel. Abel was a shepherd and occupied himself with the life that was already there. He is the symbol of the inborn divine force which works in man as the wisdom which he does not acquire himself, which flows into him. Cain creates something new out of what the world offers. He represents the passive masculine wisdom, which must at first be fertilized from the outside, which goes out into the world to gather wisdom and to create from what has been gathered. Cain killed Abel; which means that male wisdom offers resistance against the female wisdom, since it feels that it must subdue and remodel the physical wisdom. [Read the book for more stories about Cain and Abel.]

Long ago, Freemasons thus set themselves the ideal of taking up the challenge. They wanted to use male wisdom to work against the female wisdom that was taken over by the priesthood. The great images of the Bible were to be considered intuitive female wisdom transferred to the priests, to which they wished to counterprose the wisdom self-acquired by the male. This battle against the wisdom of the priests expressed the opposition of the Freemasons. Those who took part in it had to be kept free from any influence of female wisdom. This battle was concerned with physical evolution, and it was thus necessary for the Freemasons to avoid any contact with women in relation to their work. They knew that their opposition to the female spirit could not be carried through unless they were undisturbed by female thinking....

The occult tradition embodied in Freemasonry works to bring about the reestablishment of the Lost word. It seeks to enable the introduction of the active into the passive male element, so that it can regain the procreative force in the spirit and turn what is passive into an active element, so that the Sons of Cain would be able to produce out of themselves.

Thus a tradition developed that saw the female as the primeval force. This presented everything in the world as wisdom. However, the female element lost part of the physical power to reproduction, as it was transferred to the male. Now everything re-spiritualized itself again—a process in which male power tries to grasp control for itself. In thinking, the male element seeks to outlast the female. There will come a time, however, when asexuality will be reestablished again, and the struggle will be about which of the two sexes will first attain this state of asexuality. Hence, the Freemasons endeavors to make the male sex—or to express it better, the "male spirit"—outlast the female and attain to the state of asexuality.

An occult connection exists between the power of speech and the power of sexual reproduction. The *Word* has made everything. Originally it lived in the human being, who lost it. We can no longer create independently because we no longer have the Word. Only those who were present at creation can know it.... Whoever wants to regain the power of procreation must gain possession of the Word. The truly creative power must unite itself with the Word. The Word will bring forth the human being of the future....

We have seen why these spiritual currents [the priestly female–Abel versus the Freemason male–Cain] run parallel to each other. Therefore, we can also understand the significance of the anthroposophic movement. In the spiritual realm, it is preparing, what will happen later on physically—that is, the reunion of the sexes. Divided wisdom must likewise flow together again as *one* divine wisdom. Through anthroposophic wisdom, a balance must be found in human beings, between the religious priestly wisdom and the wisdom of the Freemasonry. The wisdom of the future must be brought from the higher human, which lives equally in male and female. To develop what is needed and what is completely uninfluenced by things of the physical plane is the purpose of the anthroposophic movement.

Anthroposophy [*anthropos* = human; *Sophia* = wisdom] is truly male–female wisdom, which is valid equally for both sexes. Through the teaching of reincarnation [we incarnate once as one sex then as the other approximately every 2,160 years], we recognize that it is not the personality of a particular Earth life that is expressed in each new earthly life; rather, the causal body, or entelechy, creates itself asexually.

Once we become aware of this, we become spiritually enlivened with something higher than sexuality and independent of the causes of conflict between the two currents.[76]

Now that everything is clear, we need to meditate on these remarkable comments. This is the only place I have found any understanding of the separation of man and woman. When I reflect on these words, I get a better understanding of modern life and the gender revolution brewing in the world.

In Assisi I spend much of my two days walking and soaking up the Sun's rays, sitting on rock walls, tower walls, church steps, terraces, fountains, and benches and visiting cafés, museums, and churches, admiring and absorbing another period of human history.

I discover a restaurant overlooking the plain and the town with its lovely red tiled roof and enjoy supper while watching the Sun warm the skies with carmines that become soft shades of sienna as it sets. In the restaurant are a young Japanese couple, older American couples, and priests with their English relatives. The waiters work feverishly to accommodate the diners, who sip wine with the pasta dishes, followed by rich, black coffee and dessert.

After a long day of taking in many great works of art, I go to bed in a small, clean, friendly bed and breakfast on the upper east end of town.

If I were to tell others what I was really doing, they would think I am super-religious. Although I visit painting after painting of Madonnas and numerous scenes from the bible and the life of Christ, I am far from religious. I was not raised in a devout family, even though we were Catholics. My parents never went to church, saying that those who go to church on Sunday speak badly of one another as soon as they came out. My mother called them hypocrites. We were brought up in an atmosphere free of religion, except for a bit of catechism when we were young. We went to church sporadically, and on such occasions my two sisters and I would sit in the back and enjoy singing, or, more accurately, yelling out the songs.

---

76 Rudolf Steiner, *The Temple Legend*, pp 229–238 (translation revised).

At the age of twelve, I was told not to bite the host, so I said I will bite it, and if nothing happens this is all false. The sky, of course, did not fall on me, and I quit going to church or believing in anything. That must have been the beginning of my agnosticism, which became an interest in Zen during my ten years of studying martial arts with several Okinawan Masters (I received a black belt when I was twenty). Then I became an atheist in my early twenties, a time when I visited as many churches in France as I could. Buddhism then caught my attention, and I studied Vipassana with the Buddhist master Goenka during seven annual ten-day meditation retreats of noble silence.

After this, I took a detour into the Muslim faith while living in Tehran, where I married a Persian from a Muslim family. I was especially interested in the more spiritual side of Islam, such as Sufism. I also studied Taoism and Hinduism and began deep studies in Anthroposophy during my late thirties, which returned me to my Christian roots and a much greater understanding of those teachings, as well as the other major religions.

Six hundred years ago, I would have been considered a heretic and possibly burned at the stake for such explorations. The remarkable knowledge we have available today is the result of the martyrdom of many great thinkers who paid dearly for thinking so freely. Thanks to them, we can believe or not, freely choose a denomination or religion, proclaim oneself as an agnostic, atheist, or anything else from today's smorgasbord of belief systems. When I read the works of philosophers, thinkers, and devout men and women, I am always thankful for their words, which are heavy with suffering that calls for a special mood of reverence.

What I find living in most of the paintings I've seen in Italy is untouchable and invisible, and I have been living with this for several weeks now. Goethe, with his keen skills of observation, puts it in the most remarkable way:

> At present I am preoccupied with sense-impressions to which no book or picture can do justice. The truth is that, in putting my powers of observation to the test, I have found a new interest in life. How far will my

scientific and general knowledge take me? Can I learn to look at things with clear, fresh eyes? How much can I take in at a single glance? Can the grooves of old mental habits be effaced? This is what I am trying to discover. The fact that I have to look after myself keeps me mentally alert all the time and I find that I am developing a new elasticity of mind. I have become accustomed to only having to think, will, give orders and dictate, but now I have to occupy myself with the rate of exchange, changing money, paying bills, taking notes and writing with my own hand.

From Bolzano to Trento one travels for nine miles through a country which grows ever more fertile. Everything which, higher up the mountains, must struggle to grow, flourishes here in vigor and health, the Sun is bright and hot and one can believe again in a God....

The noble objects with which I am surrounded never lose their freshness for me. I did not grow with them. I have not wrung from each its peculiar secret. Some attract me so powerfully that, for a while, I become indifferent, even unjust, to others. For example the Pantheon, the Apollo Belvedere one or two colossal heads and, recently the Sistine Chapel have so obsessed me that I see almost nothing else. But how can we petty as we are and accustomed to pettiness, ever become equal to such noble perfection? Even when one has adjusted oneself to some degree, a tremendous mass of new things crowd in on one, facing one at every step, each demanding the tribute of one's attention. How is one to find one's way through? Only by patiently allowing it all to grow slowly inside one, and by industriously studying what others have written for one's benefit....

On me, the ultimate effect of this tour was to strengthen my sense of really standing on classic soil and convince my senses and my spirit that her greatness was, is and ever will be. It lies in the nature of time and the mutual interaction of physical and moral forces that greatness and splendor must perish, but my ultimate feeling was less of sadness at all that had been destroyed than of joy at so much which had been preserved and even reconstructed more splendidly than it had been before....

The observation that all greatness is transitory should not make us despair; on the contrary, the realization that the past was great should stimulate us to create something of consequence ourselves, which, even when, in its turn, it has fallen in ruins, may continue to inspire our descendants to a noble activity such as our ancestors never lacked....

I am now in a state of clarity and calm such as I had not known for a long time. My habit of looking at and accepting things as they are without pretension is standing me in good stead and makes me secretly very happy. Each day brings me some new remarkable objects, some

A nun in Assisi

Two views of La Basilica di San Francesco, Assisi

new great picture, and a whole city which the imagination will never encompass, however long one thinks and dreams.

Today I went to the pyramid of Cestius and in the evening climbed to the top of the Palatine, where the ruins of the imperial palaces stand like rocks. It is impossible to convey a proper idea of such things. Nothing here is mediocre, and if, here and there, something is in poor taste, it, too, shares in the general grandeur.

When I indulge in self-reflection, as I like to do occasionally, I discover in myself a feeling which gives me great joy. Let me put it like this. In this place, whoever looks seriously about him and has eyes to see is bound to become a stronger character: he acquires a sense of strength hitherto unknown to him.

His soul receives the seal of a soundness, a seriousness without pedantry, and a joyous composure. At least, I can say that I have never been so sensitive to the things of this world as I am here. The blessed consequences will, I believe, affect my whole future life.

So let me seize things one by one as they come; they will sort themselves out later. I am not here simply to have a good time, but to devote myself to the noble objects about me, to educate myself before I reach forty.[77]

The late-night train ride back to Florence was pleasant and included stops for coffee and a few hours to ponder the riches I had been fortunate enough to see and live with for a few hours. Today I worked all morning and planned to have lunch after shopping at the village stores. I bought fresh pesto sauce, salami, lettuce, and fresh bread for a lunch on the terrace overlooking Florence. The distant southeastern mountains are shrouded by a warm autumn haze, and since I have been in Italy, my friends the olives have had time to ripen. They are becoming a rich black and will soon be harvested. They taste extremely bitter and need to be cured before they are edible, but the olives here are for making the rich olive oil that I sprinkle profusely over my salads. The remainder of the day is spent writing and studying to the

---

77 Goethe, *Italian Journey* (New York: Penguin, 1962), tr. Herzfeld and Sym, pp. 38, 148, 434–435, 136–137.

sounds of operas being played upstairs. The family is made up of aficionados of opera.

Another day passes, and I return to the Basilica di Santa Croce, which I had not seen properly. The area has a more lived-in atmosphere, with lots of upper-class bed and breakfasts for the wealthier tourists, nice restaurants. Here one can actually meet the Florentines shopping and enjoying their city. On the way, near Santa Croce, I stopped in a leather shop and bought a work of art, a purse handmade and decorated by a Jewish brother-and-sister team.

> The stones and materials used for the construction came from the demolition of the city's second circle of walls, on whose outskirts a new zone had emerged to the east, inhabited by a large number of poor families, as well as by the new rich: a densely populated suburb characterized by the presence of commercial, mercantile, and banking activities. It was here that the woolen cloth exported all over the world was dyed (refences to this industry can still be found in the names of the streets, such as Via dei Tintori); here that woolen and silk fabrics were woven (Via dei Tessitori); here lived all the people who had moved into the city from the countryside to work in the textile industry, along with bankers, the Peruzzi and Bardi and other powerful families (Baroncelli, Rinuccini, Alberti), who had grown rich on the proceeds of the industry. So it is easy to understand why the Franciscans, a mendicant order, chose this site outside the second circle of the city walls to erect its Florentine church, located at the center of a newly developed zone with whose inhabitants it was necessary to communicate in a clear language: a language that could be understood by the emerging middle class, the "nouveaux riches," and the poor alike.[78]

I am glad I went back to this church, because Santa Croce has so much to take in, especially the frescoes and icons by my favorite painters and sculptors, Donatello, Rossellinom Desiderio de Settignano, Bartolini, and others. I was able to take lots of pictures and never tire of seeing these sacred paintings.

> Right from the start, Santa Croce had been conceived as a giant book in which the stories of the Gospels could be read through simple and clear images comprehensible to all. The technique used to represent the scenes from the life of Christ and St. Francis was the cheapest and the most effective: painting the walls with fresco.[79]

---

78 Antonio Paolucci, *Sacred Florence*, p. 134.
79 Ibid.

The colors are amazing, of course, and many of the frescoes have been touched up or repainted, but the effect is still there. It was awkward to see monuments dedicated to famous men who were persecuted in their own time by the Church or city state. Galileo lived under house arrest, and now we see a sumptuous monument in his name. Dante, who was expelled from Florence, also has a monument.

Some of my favorites are frescoes in the Baroncelli Chapel, which depict scenes from the life of the Virgin, and an icon by Giotto, *Coronation of the Virgin*. I find them endearing because they are very simple and taken from daily life and seem very modern in design. Also *Annunciation to the Shepherds* by Taddeo Gaddi, painted in soft grays, dark grays, indigo, and an eerie yellow light. The shepherd is looking at an angel in the sky as his sheep sleep peacefully at his feet and a loving dog points his nose toward the angel as if to smell his presence. Nothing is superfluous in the composition; details from real life are exquisitely earthy in a matter-of-fact way. This is but one little fresco out of hundreds in this magnificent church.

Another masterpiece is the Rinuccini Chapel with "Scenes from the Life of Mary Magdalene" and "Scenes from the Life of the Virgin" by Giovanni di Milano (1365) and other Giotto school painters. My words are not sufficient to describe the splendor of these living "books" on walls, but I find that the words of Hildegard of Bingen (ca. 1112) capture the sacred images, the holy atmosphere in which these painters, artists, sculptors breathed and worked.

> It was *Matthew* who taught people lightly and sweetly through the mildness of his thought and without any abrasion of mind. In every way he strengthened the teaching of the apostles and acknowledged it, as the model of his own method of instruction. And thus, he converted young people in true faith to God by his preaching, which trickled down to them as deliciously as honey. Because of the gentleness of his way of life, people accepted his teaching just the way an infant sucks milk. Indeed, the Holy spirit influenced him in such a way that he gave an accurate account of the incarnation of a God's Son. Mathew prepared himself a garment made from silk of good intentions, that is, from a righteous contrition. And just as daylight prepares the way for brightness, he applied all these things to justice, and for sake of justice he did not avoid martyrdom.
>
> By way of contrast, *Thomas* upheld for people a strict and difficult morality through his own conduct. He did not undertake anything

frivolously and did not come to agreement easily, but he believed what he had seen. Anything that was not visible, however, he grasped only through the evidence of outer signs. And thus signs are known through deeds because bodily things are seen in a bodily way, while spiritual things are grasped in a spiritual way. Men and women, as well, are known as spiritual beings by the holiness of their deeds. In this way Thomas converted many people to God. He gave justice a long gown of green silk, which as worn over a white garment, and this gown shone with the brilliance of the Sun. By the rectitude of his good intentions he adorned justice and caused it to outshine every other source of light. He converted the hearts of unbelievers from idolatry to God, and offered himself in martyrdom for the sake of the Ruler of the universe.

Peter, on the other hand, wove a cloak out of scarlet linen, for he expressed rectitude, mildness, and severity. In this way he adored justice for all classes of Church members and subjected himself to all types of sorrow—both of body and soul.

Mathias was kind and humble—just like a dove. He kept aloof from the changeableness of human affairs as well as from envy and hate. He was a vessel of the Holy Spirit, which dwells in those who do not let their spirit roam about the streets and gaze idly at everything in sight. In addition, he performed many signs and wonders in the sight of believers and unbelievers—and he performed these works in humility—just as if he did not know what he was doing. He longed for martyrdom as if for a banquet. In this way he prepared for justice a royal throne from which it might rule in all dignity. The heads of eagles and the feet of lions supported his throne on four pillars, while Mathias flew about the four corners of the world in humility; no kind of injustice could overcome him. Far and wide he preached and for this reason suffered patiently much hardship. Yet he completed manfully all that he did. Therefore, people listened to him with pleasure and loved him exceedingly. By his humility he caused justice to take its seat upon the throne he had prepared for it. In this way God chose the twelve apostles with all their different characteristics, just as he had chosen the twelve prophets. For God is marvelous.

Afterward, God discovered a tiny spark and stirred it up with the divine fire. This fire is *Paul* in whom God achieved many wondrous deeds. God completes the divine signs both in stormy and active individuals as well as in gentle individuals so that people will not turn away and say that God carries out the divine wonders only in mild individuals.[80]

---

80 Matthew Fox, ed., *Hildegard of Bingen's Book of Divine Works: With Letters and*

This was the world the artists lived in, and their brushes painted what was living in their soul.

The cloister adjacent to Santa Croce includes the Pazzi Chapel by architect Filippo Brunelleschi, a comfort to the eyes and the soul.

> Brunelleschi was among the first architects of the Renaissance to defend classical principles of symmetry and proportion in architectural design.... In the graceful little chapel he produced for the Pazzi family of Florence...it is in the interior that Brunelleschi's break with the medieval past is fully realized.... The repetition of geometric shapes enforces a new kind of visual clarity...a sense of order and harmony that is unsurpassed in Early renaissance architecture....
>
> Brunelleschi's enthusiasm for an architecture of harmonious proportions was shared by his younger colleague [Leon Battista Alberti]....
>
> Both Alberti and Brunelleschi espoused the Hellenic theory that the human form mirrored the order inherent in the universe. The human microcosm was the natural expression of the divine macrocosm. Accordingly, the study of nature and the understanding and exercise of its underlying harmonies put one in touch with the macrocosm. Rational architecture, reflecting natural laws, would help cultivate rational individuals. Just as the gentle modes in music elicited refined behavior, so harmoniously proportioned buildings might produce ideal citizens.[81]

Rudolf Steiner offers a different perspective:

> You might now wish to point out that you do not, in fact, do any adding up when you see an ellipse. This is true, but your astral body does; what the geometrician does consciously the astral body [the body of feelings] does unconsciously, for it is a fully-trained geometrician. You have no idea at all of the knowledge that is contained in your astral body. In it you are an immensely learned geometrician, only of course the geometry you know in your astral body can only be brought into consciousness with considerable effort. Everything is present down there in your astral body, and if those who teach geometry could instead utilize a pump they would no longer have a need for their usual teaching methods. The knowledge would well up of its own accord. We add, then, the two distances from the foci and always get the same result [about the two foci in the ellipse]. what does it really mean when we find beauty in an

---

Songs (Rochester, VT: Bear & Company, 1987), vision 9.
81 Gloria K. Fiero, *The Humanistic Tradition*, Book 2, p. 53.

ellipse? It means that our astral body is adding up and the sum total is always the same. Imagine yourself adding up without knowing it and every time getting the same answer. You feel pleased. From this point you get the same result, and then from that one again, and this fills you with delight. This is the living experience of the ellipse.

In the case of the circle there is no such feeling of delight, for the circle is so immediately obvious. The ellipse causes us greater pleasure because there we have to be inwardly active. The more active we are inwardly, the greater the pleasure we experience. People find it difficult to realize that the inner human being craves activity. It is only in people's conscious life that they wish to be lazy. The astral body is not only wiser, but also more industrious and would like to remain active all the time.[82]

Steiner approaches architecture from yet another, even more potent perspective. The implications are far-reaching.

However much study may be devoted to the elimination of crime and wrong-doing in the world, true redemption, turning evil into goodness, will depend in future on whether true art and architecture are able to generate a certain cultural atmosphere, one that can fill the hearts and souls of human beings—if they allow this atmosphere to influence them—so that liars will cease to lie and disturbers of the peace will cease to interfere with the peace of their fellow citizens. Buildings will begin to speak. They will speak a language of which people today have no inkling.

Today, people gather in congresses to negotiate world peace. They imagine that speaking and listening can actually create harmony and peace, but peace and harmony will never be established in this way. Peace and harmony and conditions worthy of humanity cannot be established unless the gods speak to us. And when will the gods speak to us?

We had better ask first: When do human beings speak to us? They speak when they have a larynx. Human beings would be unable to speak without a larynx. What the nature gods have given in our larynx we are able to pass on to the whole world if we find appropriate artistic forms, and the gods will speak to us through such forms. We need only understand how we can enter this great process....

Art is the creation of organs through which the gods will be able to speak to humankind.[83]

---

82 Rudolf Steiner, Architecture as a Synthesis of the Arts, pp. 105–106.
83 Ibid., pp. 82–83.

After spending most of the morning in the church and the monastery, I go for my usual coffee around the piazza. It is a busy lunch break, and I have another lesson in coffee while eating my sandwich. The waiters are very patient with us tourists. I order a cappuccino, and then someone wants a caffè macchiato, espresso with only whipped milk on it. Mine is espresso with fluffy milk on top and milk. Then there is caffè marochino, a macchiato topped with chocolate powder. I ask the waiter how much coffee he sells in a day, and he tells me from twelve to fifteen kilograms, or up to thirty pounds of coffee. This amount multiplied by the number of cafés in Italian cities and villages produces an astronomical figure. This is, of course, great for the countries that grow coffee. The waiter tells me that they purchase coffee from all over the world, and that they roast and blend the beans at the café. This café serves one of the nicest cups of coffee around.

 I enjoy watching people eat and drink. Some first eat the fluffy milk with a spoon, then drink the coffee. Men tend to drink the more "manly" straight espresso and scoop up the sugary residue at the bottom. Some rush into the café as though it is an emergency to get a caffeine fix. Older women order everything—espresso, fluffy cream, and chocolate—and savor it to the last drop. The barista who makes the coffee is very proud to say that in Italy one takes the coffee-making business very seriously. One just cannot visit Italy and not drink this delightful beverage. Gerbert Grohman offered some interesting facts about coffee: the plant vol. 2 p. 165:

> A very important member of the *Rubiaceae* for modern civilization is *coffee*. It is a native of the primeval forest of the highlands of Abyssinia. From there it made its way to Arabia and thence to Europe and the rest of the world. Today there are other varieties in cultivation, not only *coffee arabica*. There is, for instance, *Liverian* coffee from the west coast of Africa. It was impossible to stop the spread of the much-desired beverage, although it met with strong opposition. The first coffee house was opened in Constantinople [Istanbul] in 1517, but in 1523 we are told that the Grand Vizier of Constantinople—Kuproli—ordered that anyone caught drinking coffee should be sewn up in a leather sack and thrown into the sea. Coffee drinkers were threatened with the severest punishment and even with the pains of Hell by secular and spiritual authorities. Flogging

also was of no avail. Even much later Liselotte von der Pfalz wrote in a letter: "My God, how can something so bitter and stinking as coffee be enjoyable. We had a red-faced Archbishop from Paris, whose breath stank just like coffee, which makes me shudder when I smell the stuff." Goethe's aversion to coffee-drinking is also known. The state opposed coffee on economic grounds. It had to be imported and paid for with good money. If in such a comparatively short time a stimulant assumes such importance in spite of such opposition, there must be a reason.

Coffee stimulates the peristaltic action of the intestine, because the rhythmic side of the metabolism is enhanced. The excretory processes in the intestines, kidneys, and sweat glands are heightened. All the rhythmic processes including the action of the blood in the metabolism are enlivened. All these symptoms are due to the heightened action of the astral body. There is also the fact of a certain conformity in the chemical structure of coffee and uric acid. So we see that the physiology of the action of coffee gives the same picture as the plant that produces the stimulant.[84]

When I watch the baristas make the coffee, they resemble caffeine. They "become" the coffee I suppose after serving it all day and probably drinking it, too. They never sit still but are always busy cleaning the already-clean counter over and over again. They slam the machine, empty the cups, add more coffee, froth the milk, wash the cups, and so on all day long. They know only two speeds—fast and faster. Even when no one is around, they rush around. The baristas usually have a little mustache or some other type of facial hair, always nicely trimmed. They never look the least bit unkempt in their crisp white aprons. After viewing paintings of Madonnas and Christ all day, I watch the guys who serve coffee. My daughter would say that this creates balance.

I get up very early the next day to go to a couple of hill towns about fifty miles southeast of Florence. I'd seen them from the train when I went to Assisi. They are Arezzo and Cortona. I arrive around 9;30, and the village simpleton helps

---

84 Gerbert Grohmann, *The Plant*, p. 165.

A café

me find the bus to go up the hill, saving me an hour's walk. Cortina is a lovely fortress town, with beautiful churches, cathedrals, a piazza, and lovely, renovated stone houses everywhere. There is also a fortress on top of the hill and many convents. It has the feeling of an artistic town, and I see many young couples with children, as well as a lot of artisan activities. As usual, I find the most beautiful frescoes in the churches, some of which I was not supposed to photograph, though some I manage to capture.

I go into the Etruscan museum to see artifacts that speak of long ago. I love the little female statuette with the Sun's rays as a hat on their heads, with its complement the Mars male warrior. What a people they were! The area abounds with Etruscan sites. Their golden jewelry was priceless—so long ago, women adorned themselves with Sun-like jewels.

These towns are rich in culture, one on top of the other. One cannot ignore where we have been, Etruscans, Greeks, Romans, all there for us to see and feel. I find that, after wandering around so many of these beautiful hill towns, there is a strong sense of civility that I do not encounter in other parts of Europe. Ancient, and medieval architects knew how to plan a city using universal laws, and this is reflected in all these villages and towns. One feels that they are made for human beings to live together, to meet and enjoy the surroundings. Towns are often situated on very sacred sites and special places where the Gods could speak to them; or high on a hill to be nearer to the clouds and enjoy a spectacular view of the landscape; or next to a sacred spring where water meets earth; or amid a special meadow of special plants or an oak grove. Their designs worked with nature, because they were still alive to that realm in those days, and the elders were members of mystery schools involved with designing buildings and temples and planning cities and roads. One feels this in many places here. The piazzas often rest on an old Roman theater or on even older Etruscan or Greek sites, and the senses become more alive in such towns. We are still the beneficiaries of the ancient sacred knowledge.

I walk to the top of Cortona along an old Roman road shaded by olive and cypress trees. A cathedral dominates the town and several smaller ones below. Overlooking the whole area is a fortress, where one can gaze for miles and miles. On the way up, I visit a small chapel in which nuns perform their noontime rituals, seemingly unconcerned with the affairs of this world. Continuing on, I walk to the edge of town at the top of the hill, where the small road passes under the arch of the old fort. From there I see far and wide into the distant hills. After feasting on juicy golden grapes, I go back down into the tiny streets. Some of the houses have tiny, terraced gardens with fig trees, which, to my chagrin, I cannot reach. There are also a few small vineyards of red grapes.

The town is not overwhelmed by tourists and has a lovely feeling to it. I sense that Italy is exceptionally alive, especially in the countryside, perhaps because of the olive trees and vineyards throughout the area that require constant, loving attention. The locals seem steeped in tradition. They are almost fanatical about their foods, wines, and inimitable cooking techniques. They bathe in sunshine that does not exist for those in the north. The people here have not separated themselves from nature and the land nor abandoned the countryside as they have in France and Spain. Everywhere here, the land is well cared for; fields of corn have been harvested, and the farmers are turning the rich, sienna or golden-ochre earth under. The sunflowers, too, have been

Overlooking Arezzo

harvested. When people are surrounded by well-planned architecture and farms, they are less tempted to let go of what they love so much in exchange for more superficial modern surroundings. Many generations have cared for what I see all around. Where I live in the American Midwest, no one has any concern for the scenery, and most of the U.S. is quickly becoming an eyesore. This happens in Italy, too, but it is far less widespread.

Steiner once mentioned that people learn to be civil and more human through the architecture they look at.[85] When buildings are not well planned or are built helter-skelter, as is frequently done, it is absorbed by people, who tend to become less moral, as they are constantly surrounded by an amoral landscape. Here in Italy, people are surrounded by sacred and meaningful architecture, and their lives seem to reflect it. For example, the trains and buses operate on a kind of honor system. I can take a bus without a ticket and not pay. No one checks. I must check myself. It does not occur to people here not to pay. I find a sense of honesty here. (Of course, I am not talking about

---

85 *Architecture as a Synthesis of the Arts.*

A typical reclining figure on an Etruscan cinerary urn (left) and an ancient mother/goddess

politics and taxes.) In other places such as France or Germany, one cannot take a bus without a ticket. Moreover, driving in Italy seems to be wholly chaotic, but I find that people are for the most part careful with one another.

With these thoughts in mind, perhaps architects of the future should take more responsibility for their designs and not be governed only by the material aspects of their trade.

I take the bus from Cortona to Arezzo, a pleasant ride through the countryside. The kids are coming out of schools, getting on the bus, and fooling around like all kids do. The countryside here is more populated, and soon we arrive on the outskirts of Arezzo. It is on a hill and the outskirts spread out more than in Cortona.

I visit the Basilica di San Francesco, where I find the fresco cycle "The History of the True Cross" on three walls of the Cappella Maggiore. I cannot take pictures but do spend a long time immersed in it. This great work by Piero della Francesca is simply amazing and looks very Byzantine. The people's faces are done with a loveliness and warmth that gives them a strong presence. A huge twelfth-century crucifix hangs at the front, which Piero may have contemplated as he painted his frescoes around 1452.

> The subject matter of the stories...is drawn from Jacopo da Varazze's *Golden Legend,* a thirteenth-century text that recounts the miraculous story of the wood of Christ's Cross....

The story tells how Adam, on his deathbed, sends his son Seth to Archangel Michael, who gives him some seedlings from the tree of original sin to be placed in his father's mouth at the moment of his death. The tree that grows on the patriarch's grave is chopped down by King Solomon and its wood, which could not be used for anything else, is thrown across a stream to serve as a bridge. The Queen of Sheba, on her journey to see Solomon and hear his words of wisdom, is about to cross the stream, when by a miracle she learns that the Savior will be crucified on that wood. She kneels in devout adoration. When Solomon discovers the nature of the divine message received by the Queen of Sheba, he orders that the bridge be removed and the wood, which will cause the end of the kingdom of the Jews, be buried. But the wood is found and, after a second premonitory message, becomes the instrument of the Passion. Three centuries later, just before the battle of Monte Milvio against Maxentius, Emperor Constantine is told in a dream that he must fight in the name of the Cross to overcome his enemy. After Constantine's victory, his mother Helena travels to Jerusalem to recover the miraculous wood. No one knows where the relic of the Cross is, except a Jew called Judas, who refuses to reveal the secret. Judas is tortured in a well and finally confesses that he knows of a temple dedicated to Venus where the three crosses of Calvary are hidden. Helena orders that the temple be destroyed; the three crosses are found and the True Cross is recognized because it causes the miraculous resurrection of a dead youth. In the year 615, the Persian King Khosrow steals the wood, setting it up as an object of worship amidst idolatrous symbols. The Eastern emperor Heraclitus wages war on the Persian King and, having defeated him, returns to Jerusalem with the Holy Wood. But a divine power prevents the Emperor from making his triumphal entry into Jerusalem. So Heraclitus, setting aside all pomp and magnificence, enters the city carrying the Cross in a gesture of humility, following Jesus Christ's example.

Very briefly, this is the basic narrative account of the 'Story of the Cross'. It is hardly surprising that this rather naïve tale was used so frequently as a source in late-fourteenth-century Tuscan paintings.[86]

The story is rich in Eastern legends and would have appealed to the more humanistic, scholarly patrons of art. "The Story of the Cross" was also painted around 1380 by Gaddi for the Franciscans in the Church of Santa Croce in Florence.

---

86 Alessandro Angelini, *Piero della Francesca* (Florence: Scala/Riverside, 1985), p. 22.

Walking up one of the streets, I come into a large, slanted cobblestone piazza, where I see a most unusual church in the twelfth-century Romanesque style, Santa Maria della Pieve. It is very austere inside, an atmosphere enhanced by the music of a woman practicing on the organ. I stay and listen for a couple of hours.

There are few people in the church, so I can just sit and watch and listen. On the altar is a splendid triptych, a Madonna and child, which I photograph. The church is magnificent in its simplicity—no frescoes or paintings or anything except the cold stones. Nonetheless, the high walls and the columns are adorned at the top with unusual "stone frescoes" depicting various pagan nature figures and primitive plant scenes. I could have spent the whole afternoon there absorbed in these ancient designs which appear to come from another realm.

> The human condition of being bound to Earth is expressed by a shape that has a wide base and runs upward to a point. Sensing these forces, people felt that they were standing on the Earth.
>
> In a similar way, they also became aware of their connection with the Sun. The Sun works downward toward the Earth, and they expressed this by portraying the lines of forces raying inward, just as the Sun, in its apparent journey round the Earth, sends its rays down toward a mid-point....

> Initially this force, or cosmic tension of Earth and Sun, was felt and only later did people begin to consider how they might portray it. The best medium for the purposes of artistic expression proved to be a plant or tree whose forms run upward to a point from a wide base, alternatively with palms. Plants having a form like a wide bud were alternated with palms. The palms represented the Sun's forces, and the Earth forces by bud forms running upward to a point.

People learned to feel their position within the cosmos and created, so to speak, certain form relationships. Subsequently, on reflection, they selected certain plants as a means of expression, instead of having to create artistic objects for the purpose. The choice of suitable plants was the artistically creative act that was in turn the result of a living experience of cosmic connection. Thus the creative urge in human beings is no mere wish to imitate things in the surrounding world. Artistic representation of natural things became an aspect of art only at a later stage. When people no longer realized that palms were used to express the Sun forces, they began to think that the ancients had simply imitated palms in their designs. This was never the case; the people of antiquity used the leaves of the palms because they typified the Sun forces. All true artistic creation has arisen from a superabundance of forces in human nature—forces that cannot find expression in outer life and that strive to do so through our consciousness of being connected with the universe as a whole.[87]

As if I had not taken in enough, I encounter another large church, Arezzo Cathedral, with its whole ceiling painted in frescoes, though too high to really appreciate, as well as mesmerizing stained-glass windows all around, especially the front window. It had one panel of the Madonna in a light carmine with a strip of mauve on a coat of lapis, surrounded by an emerald-green coat, dotted with yellow stars and held by angels. It is the most healing green and lapuz blue I've ever seen. The Madonna is just one of the many figures on this immense work. I find the colors comforting. The church has so much of everything else that it doesn't need the usual myriad of paintings. One can breathe and not be stifled by too much art. Only the dome was painted, like some others, for the angels because it's too far up for humans to see.

I still wished to see Casa del Petrarca, believed to be the birthplace of Francesco Petrarca (1304–1374). I meditated a bit and looking at Francesco's handsome face, as well as the hundreds of antique books.

---

[87] Rudolf Steiner, *Architecture as a Synthesis of the Arts*, pp. 59–60 (translation revised).

The façade of Santa Maria della Pieve (above)
Woman practicing the organ (below)

Interior arches of Santa Maria della Pieve (above)
An alter piece (below)

Following a hard day of travel, I decide to stay in Florence for the next day and visit the Palazzo Medici Riccardi and the Capella dei Magi, with frescoes by Benozzo Gozzoli (c. 1421–1497), one of my favorites. He was born west of Florence to a family of farmers and worked with Fra Angelico during his younger years.

Again no photography is allowed. It was agony not to be able to take something of this beauty home, so I bought a book—better than nothing. The chapel is stunning, large frescoes on all sides. In those days, no one but the Medici's and their friends got to see these paintings or spend time in these luxurious settings. I have never seen such splendid work anywhere, and it was worth the € 15 entry fee.

The rest was not so great, but they were exhibiting a bronze statue rescued from the sea. What a project that had been! The statue stood there in its original glory, and I remained for a long time contemplating that magnificent sculpture of the human body. In my twenties I made a lot of nude charcoal drawings of the human body in classes. We had all sorts of models—dancers, young and old men and women, black-skinned, light-skinned—each one a challenge. However, seeing this depiction of the human body in its perfect form (an Olympian gymnast after a competition), I longed for my charcoal pencils—but I did have my camera. It brings to mind a passage:

> The most perfect of all that God created for the human being is the body. The body of the human being is the most perfect form created by God. It is a tool through which the human soul looks out into the world. The human body is equipped in a wonderful way. The human body should be a temple for the soul. But the soul is not yet perfect. It is just beginning to be developed. The human body makes no mistakes; it is the imperfect soul that is constantly making mistakes. Passions, instinctive drives and desires live in the soul, and they use the body in order to satisfy these desires.[88]

The only drawback is that this sculpture had nothing to do with the rest of the place. The mix-and-match arrangement destroys the setting and atmosphere of the chapel itself. It loses some of the beauty and magnificence of the chapel and its glorious frescoes, which seem desecrated. If the original

---

88 Rudolf Steiner, *Esoteric Lessons, 1904–1909* (Great Barrington, MA: SteinerBooks, 2007), p. 108.

The piazza in Arezzo

painter was here to see this, I am sure he would be unhappy with the results. Nonetheless, words cannot describe the frescoes. Though they have been totally redone, the work is splendid, a living picture.

I could have stayed there all day. Now I look at the book and see that it is not so well done. The pictures, however, are like a movie; during the fifteenth century, the frescoes *were* the movies of the day. Most people could not read, so they learned stories of saints, various scholars, or the Old and New testaments through these frescoes. Today, we are no longer sensitive to such moving, lively story images. They are still alive, like so much of this sacred art. The artists lived what they painted, so that those looking at it can become immersed in what is alive. But one must have some feeling to live in such pictures. This is the most striking thing about all these paintings and frescoes; they are still alive. As I stood in that little chapel along with ten others, we were stunned by the sight. The horses looked like they could run us over, and we felt as though we were actually in the procession portrayed, instantly living in those times. The pictures are truthful—everyone there felt it—but we could not stay as long as we wished; another ten people were waiting.

I moved on... another sunny, busy day in the city.

While wandering, I discovered a ceramic shop owned by a Persian couple. I spoke Persian with the woman, an artist, and it was nice to be in such an artisan shop so far from Esfahan, Iran. They had a workshop at a farm in the countryside and were selling their beautiful ceramics to people from around the world. I would have loved to buy a scene for my bathroom.

At a bus station, I inquired about my next day trip, which would take me to San Gimignano, a town of fourteen towers of various heights; there used to be thirty-five of them. The towers are very high, and it is said that during those earlier times one could travel above from tower to tower without using the street, as there were so many.

I finally got to San Gimignano on Saturday, but because of bad connections it took all morning. While waiting for a bus between towns, I had a nice chat with a group of Brazilians who were visiting relatives in Italy. It was a beautiful trip, with the scenery of Tuscan farms and villas perched atop soft hillsides and fortresses here and there among small villages. There were also a lot of vineyards, along with olive groves and the cypresses planted near homes and farms. I could spot ripe pomegranates growing on thin, bushy trees behind a stone wall. The bus climbed to the town perched on a hilltop, its towers silhouetted on the horizon. As I walked through the walled town, I passed under numerous lovely arches. The towers can be seen everywhere from all angles. The town also has lovely piazzas for lingering and entertainment from local musicians. There I have my usual espresso drink. I have now joined the group who order macchiatos instead of cappuccinos, drinking it while standing and chatting with whoever is around.

Cathedrals and churches await. The San Gimignano church is full of frescoes on all sides, and of course I forbidden to take pictures, so again I must buy the book. My suitcase is almost impossible to lift, and to get home I have to

Bronze sculpture of a young man on display at Palazzo Medici Riccardi

A young woman making a chalk drawing of the Madonna on the piazza

take buses, trains, and planes. To make it worse, the frescoes are by my favorite painters. I try to sneak in a few pictures while the woman there is distracted, but I make a mess of it. I drop my camera, which draws the attention of the watchdog, and there go my chances. The camera appears broken but, thankfully, with a little rough handling I kind of get it functioning again.

Again I am completely taken by the frescoes—the faces, colors, movements, clothes, and expressions, as well as their monumental size and the creative execution. I reluctantly leave these treasures. Just one of these frescoes or one painting could keep me busy for a lifetime of looking and meditating. And this cathedral contains literally hundreds, each better than the other—and no photography allowed.

I climb one of the towers after visiting a museum where I could not take pictures (though I did manage a few). On top I can see far and wide as I try to imagine the town of San Gimignano filled with thirty-five or more towers. It must have been delightful to bid one's neighbor good-morning from the top of these narrow towers, which are quite high, perhaps twenty stories. I see again the many farms and vineyards on the hillsides, and of course the ubiquitous olive groves. Other tourists like myself are also enchanted by the scene.

I stop next for a bite on the sloped piazza, and then go to a wine museum on top of the hill, which has dozens of wines to sample. While walking back, I find another church. Sant'Agostino is a more somber church, and no one was around to collect money or watch, so it delighted me to take at least a hundred pictures of the sacred paintings, many again by my favorite painters. I kept snapping away, and the light was coming in from the right direction. There were paintings of the Madonna paintings by Filippo Lippi, and a whole wall was filled with frescoes depicting the birth of the Virgin. In addition, lovely music was playing—a sacred choral piece.

Next, I entered the peaceful monastery garden, where I could hear the priest's voice. I visited their bookshop and bought yet another book, feeling very happy that at least in this church the people were nice and left one alone. As I walked through the church again, I took some last-minute photos. As I left, what did I see? A small, familiar yellow sign: "No Pictures." I was stunned and quickly left with my treasures. I had snapped 230 pictures that day.

There is another aspect to the effects of paintings. I can feel quite good about it when I cannot take pictures; there is a much bigger "camera" in the world.

> [Michelangelo's] glorious paintings have affected millions of people. These paintings, however, will one day fall into dust and there will be future generations who will never see his creations. But what lived in Michelangelo's soul before his paintings took outer form, what at first existed as new creations in his soul, lives on, remains, and will appear in future stages of development and be given form. Do you know why clouds and stars appear to us today? Because there were beings in preceding eras who had thoughts of clouds and stars. Everything arises from thought creations.[89]

As I walk down the narrow cobblestone streets, I feel as though I could go on like this for another ten years, looking at more and more beautiful paintings, sculptures, palaces, villas, cathedrals, and museums and never

---

89 Rudolf Steiner, *Occult Signs and Symbols* (Hudson, NY: Anthroposophic Press, 1980), p. 39.

Towers of San Gimignano

exhaust the treasures of art in this small country of Italy—and I have visited only Tuscany. With my head filled with images of sacred paintings and landscapes, I head for the bus stop to join a small army of tourists returning to Florence—the same bunch I started with early in the morning. A loud group of overweight American girls are making crude jokes and going gaga while laughing hysterically and staring at the derrière of their handsome mid-thirties and patient Italian guide. They seem to think that other people cannot understand them. Also waiting for the bus are French and English couples. Some middle-aged Italian men, probably returning from their day's work, told the American girls to shut up and not make so much noise, as they wanted to nap on the way home. It is a typical bus ride in Italy. I get back to the hills around Florence quite late. I am ready for the next day's expedition to the town of Fiesole.

I did not sleep in late the next morning. I did not want to walk the fourteen kilometers, so I take buses to Fiesole to see the Etruscan-Roman archeological site. Again the bus is filled with tourists, lots of old French couples as well as

Views of San Gimignano

Images of San Gimignano; Madonna (top)
The Passion of Christ (below) and detail, right)

Musicians busking in the piazza

Dutch, English, and Germans. We head toward the amphitheater and meander through the old fallen stones. Some people are lost in thought, some write, some simply walk. It is mysterious in a way. There are Roman baths, large pools, a great ancient temple site. We can see the whole surrounding area from here. I wonder who was worshipped here. It has a stoney silence. What did people watch in the amphitheater? A skilled orator, fights, a play, a debate?

Later I go to the bookshop and buy a book on the Etruscans. It is time for a bite to eat and a macchiato.

Everyone is waiting for the bus to see one of the sumptuous villas and a garden a few kilometers away. We pack into a van and drive along the road I had walked a few days earlier, coming from Settignano and passing my favorite fig orchard.

The gardens are my kind of gardens, with sculptures everywhere. In my garden back home I, too, have statues everywhere (copies, of course). Here there must be a hundred or more in a relatively small area. The garden is built on a steep hill, with fountains of all sizes and shapes scattered about. There

The Roman theater of Fiesole, from the beginning of the Roman imperial age and with a capacity of about 3,000 people, is still used.

are small statues, big ones, mediums ones, in the woods and by the fountains. No one lives in the huge Tuscan villa, which again seems like an abandoned monastery. I suppose it is too expansive to maintain. A non-profit organization is in charge of the grounds, and they do have a gardener. I enjoy the magnificent views overlooking the whole Florentine valley.

By the time we get back to Florence, the bus is very crowded. At the Piazza della Repubblica, a show is taking place. It is mixed martial arts, kick boxing and karate by Africans and a few Italians. It is exciting to see how they've mastered their movements, kicking in the air, somersaulting, side-kicks. I know how hard it is, because I studied karate myself. It takes a great deal of concentration, will power, and endurance of putting up with pain through many years of steady practice. These guys have tremendous control to do these flying kicks without hurting one another. The tourists are having a great time watching the performance.

I go to my final activity of the day to my favorite church and an organ concert. It is a nice way to end the day and my time here. Tomorrow morning,

I must be off to Frankfurt and then on to Chicago. Thus ends to my two months of wandering Europe, carrying many treasures inwardly as well as in my camera and laptop computer.

After spending so many hours meditating in churches, cathedrals, piazzas, buses, trains, coffee shops, markets, stairs, museums, and in front of so many sacred paintings and sculptures, gardens, roads, paths, orchards, and groves and speaking with hundreds of people from all walks of life, I enjoyed these words:

> Those whose thoughts have become living forces within through meditation are living in the divine stream. On the right, they have mere thoughts; on the left, mere perception. They exclude neither one nor the other, knowing that polarities must keep each other in balance, just as a triangle is determined by the sum of its angles.
>
> Meditation denotes surrender to thoughts and feelings that are suited especially to our individuality and with which we completely identify. It is natural for human efforts to grow weak easily on this path; it means repeatedly *overcoming* if one is to reach inner silence of the soul. With time, however, you get the feeling that until now you have merely always thought this thought; now it begins to unfold a life, an inner activity of its own. It is as if you had actually brought forth a being from yourself. The thought begins to assume an inner structure. It is an important moment when you realize that the thought only covers a certain living spiritual entity. You can thus tell yourself that your efforts have brought you to the point of providing a stage on which something may develop, that you have now awakened to its own existence. This enlivening of the meditative thought is a significant moment. You notice that the objectivity of the spirit has taken hold of you. You know that the spiritual world concerns itself with you, so to speak, that it has approached you.
>
> Something of the greatest importance takes place in selfless meditation; through the intimate process of meditating, a fine consumption of warmth is produced. Every meditation is linked with a delicate warmth and light process. Warmth and light are used up when we meditate, and this leads to a life process. In our ordinary thinking, a warmth process takes place also in our organism, and this gives rise to memory. During meditation, however, it must not come to this. If we live in pure thought content, the warmth and light that we consume inwardly is not impressed into our body, but into the general cosmic ether. This causes an outer process in our surroundings. During genuine meditation, we impress the form of our thought upon the universal ether. If in our retrospection we

The author in the garden

observe a meditation process, we are not confronted with memory but with an objective perception of the imprints in the cosmic ether.

Those who engage in true meditation live in a process that also belongs to the world. What takes place is this: during meditation, warmth is consumed, and cold thus ensues; the universal ether is cooled. Because light is also consumed, it is dimmed and darkness ensues. It is always possible for a clairvoyant to tell if a person has meditated in a location, because a shadow image of the one who meditates remains behind. It is actually cooler than the surroundings. Something has been effected that might be compared to a photographic print.

If we reflect upon this we will be able to understand how someone returning to Earth in a following earthly life still finds traces of one's meditative thoughts in the cosmic ether. Here you have a concrete example of karmic activity. As a meditator, you come increasingly to the feeling that it is not merely you and your thoughts; something transpires into which you are no doubt placed, but it also occurs outside of you as something that remains.[90]

---

90 Rudolf Steiner, *Guidance in Esoteric Training: From the Esoteric School* (London:

A martial arts display in the piazza

My flight to Frankfurt would have been uneventful, except for a black fighter jet that got in the way, forcing the pilot to put on the breaks or step on the gas—I don't know which—to avoid it. I saw the odd aircraft from the window of our plane making one of those sideways maneuvers to avoid us. Who made a mistake? Who knows? It delayed our arrival because we had to land at an airport far from Frankfurt. I finally got to my hostel after leaving all my heavy books in a locker. I discovered I would be staying smack in the middle of a brothel district that included at least twenty-five such hotels nearby. That meant no walking around at night. I stayed with the usual travelers/backpackers—one from Ireland, one from new Zealand, and some young men from Japan. The common room was full of dubious-looking men from Bulgaria or Romania who were doing funny businesses,

---

Rudolf Steiner Press, 2001), pp. 168–169 (translation revised).

and we were joined at breakfast by some women looking over-used and drawing my sympathy.

Frankfurt, the city of banks, has many skyscrapers, vaguely reminding me of San Gemignano, the city of towers in Siena, and of how the wealthiest families have always needed the tallest towers—not just for protection, but also for the sake of competition. Now we have the huge bank towers representing some of the huge companies that control the world. Meanwhile, as I walk around in one of the wealthiest cities in the world, I see old men and women drunks sleeping in the streets, drug addicts in corners, and women forced to make a living selling their bodies—many of whom appear rather sick. And the bankers, with their slick black suits and laptop computers, are out in force to make more money. In the old days, the towers communicate one to the other, while the poor down on the ground scrounge for a living. Here in Frankfurt, the tall towers *lend* one to the other, buy one another out, and still the ordinary people on the ground scrape by on a meager wage. They go to sleep with alcohol, TV, football, movies, and shopping—a modern kind of slavery. And the towers grow larger.

Once again, I visit a museum of beautiful icons in the Russian tradition and take many pictures and buy yet another book. This book has a section on icons and medicine, a topic of great interest to me. I have viewed thousands of painted images, which are my work back home as a painting therapist and a painter of healing paintings, or modern icons. We are all attracted to images, but most of us do not discriminate about which images we take in. Rudolf Steiner wrote about images; he said that it is immensely damaging to take in images without being aware of them.

Dennis Klocek, the author of *The Seer's Handbook*,[91] heads programs at Rudolf Steiner College near Sacramento. He sometimes gives his students an exercise: when you are at a supermarket, notice all the magazines that are there and sense how hungry you are for pictures. Indeed, we look at them unconsciously, especially the bad ones; we are drawn to them. And we can see their power. By becoming conscious of our wandering attention in such exercises, we can learn to control it. Another exercise is to drive around and become aware of what we look at without any real thought of what we are

---

91 *The Seer's Handbook: A Guide to Higher Perception* (Great Barrington, MA: SteinerBooks, 2005).

taking in. Pictures, Steiner says, live on in us and have a disturbing effect on our psyche, especially when they are taken in unconsciously. This is especially damaging to one's soul life.

Steiner developed many exercises to train our minds not to wander and absorb destructive images. Now imagine young people sitting in front of a television, unconsciously absorbing countless images that do damage to them as their conscious attention is diverted by tactics to sell products. They are no longer in charge of their own psyche.

Now one observes beautiful icon paintings that used to surround people during the Middle Ages, whether at home or in a local church or cathedral. They lived with these healing images of saints, scenes from the New Testament, and various depictions of the Madonna and Child; they filled people with a healthy element. Of course this is true not only of the Christian world, but also in many other cultures.

After spending so much time looking at sacred works of art, I decide to visit a museum of modern art just for a shock. I step into a cavernous, white hospital-like room that contains enormous paintings, the subject of which is nothing. They are a pell-mell mixture of images, painted poorly in painful, screaming colors. They reveal the state of the human psyche today.

> The indifference, as well as coldness, that exists toward art today arose gradually. Think of people in a modern city walking through a picture gallery or a painting exhibition. Their souls are not moved by what they see because it is unfamiliar to them. In a sense, they are faced by a multitude of riddles that they cannot solve unless they understand how the artist relates to the subject. The souls of onlookers are faced with purely individual puzzles, and the important matter is that people imagine they are solving problems related to art, but in most cases they are not grappling with the riddles of art at all, but merely with psychological problems related to the way a certain artist sees nature or views the world. Such questions, however, are not important when we examine the ages of great art, when both artist and viewer faced genuine tasks of aesthetics. The way the painting is accomplished is the real concern of the painter, whereas the substance of the painting is merely something that always flows around and thoroughly imbues the artist. You could say that today's painters are observers rather than artists; they observe the world from their particular point of view, and, owing to their particular temperament, what they happen to notice they

paint. They tackle psychological themes, problems of philosophy, or history, while the essential artistic questions of how the painting is to be approached has become almost entirely irrelevant today. People no longer have the capacity, or indeed the heart, to perceive art in its essence, which is to perceive the means and not just the content....

It is...no wonder that our age has lost the living element of soul that can sense what is really at work in the cosmos as a whole and what must flow to us from the cosmos and all its working before art can come into being. Art will never emerge from scientific concepts, let alone from abstract anthroposophic concepts. At best, these will generate insipid allegories or rigid symbols, but certainly nothing artistic. Today, thought and imagination about the world are inherently inartistic and even seek to be so.[92]

There is complete chaos in the museum. When will the phoenix be reborn amid this chaos? Of course the answer is not simply to copy the past, but to develop new icons that suit us today.

For the past six or seven weeks, I have observed and meditated on treasures of the past, and I see that we need a greater understanding about what heals, and then we need to bring it into public awareness before mass hysteria arises from mass inattention and the absorption of meaningless images viewed unconsciously. Such images are thrown at the public to take advantage of the unconsciousness.

After supper, I walk out of the restaurant opposite the main train station and encounter a female friend who had been with me six weeks earlier at a conference in Prague. Now considering all probabilities, it seems almost impossible that we meet. She had traveled throughout Germany and was now heading home. If we do not believe in some kind of higher being such as angels, how can we explain such an encounter? The answer is that we are both very much alive. One cannot explain it with earthly laws, but only with cosmic laws.

---

92 *Architecture as a Synthesis of the Arts,* pp, 135–137 (translation revised).

> Wisdom in the Spirit
> Love in the Soul
> Power in the Will:
> They guide me
> They hold me.
> I trust them
> I offer myself to them.[93]

Art must endeavor to plunge once more into the life of the elements. It has observed and studied nature long enough; it has tried long enough to solve all kinds of riddles of nature and depict, in another form, all that can be observed by penetrating nature. However, the life of the elements is dead insofar as modern art is concerned. Air, water, light—all are dead as they are painted today. Form as presented in modern sculptures is dead. A new art will be born when human souls learn to penetrate the depths of the elemental world, because that world is alive. People may argue against this; they may think that it should not be, but such arguments are only the outcome of their inertia. Either we enter the world of the elements with our whole being, absorbing the spirit and soul of the outer world and expressing it in art, or we allow art to become increasingly the work of the human soul in isolation. This could, of course, reveal many interesting things about the psychology of certain souls, but it will never lead to what only art can achieve. Such matters belong to the distant future, but we must move forward to meet the future with eyes opened by spiritual science. To do otherwise is to look into the dead and dying aspects of humanity's future.

This is why we must look for inner connections among all our forms and colors and the spiritual knowledge that moves the innermost depths of our souls. We must look for what lives in the spirit just as the Madonnas lived in Raphael, enabling him to become the painter of Madonnas. The Madonnas lived in Raphael's very being, just as they live in the educated, in the peasants in the fields, and in the artisans of his time. This is why he became the true painter of Madonnas. Until we succeed in bringing a purely artistic sense into our forms, without symbolism or allegory, all that lives in our idea of the world—not as abstract thought, dead knowledge, or science, but as living substance of the soul—until then we will not divine anything of what is described as artistic development here.[94]

---

93 Rudolf Steiner, *Isis Mary Sophia: Her Mission and Ours* (Great Barrington, MA, SteinerBooks, 2003), p. 42.
94 *Architecture as a Synthesis of the Arts*, pp, 135–137 (translation revised).

> No better love than love with no object,
> no more satisfying work than work with no purpose.
>
> If you could give up tricks and cleverness,
> that would be the cleverest trick!
>
> —Rumi[95]

Ayin, nothingness, is more existent than all the being of the world. But since it is simple, and every simple thing is complex compared with its simplicity, it is called Ayin....

The depth of primordial being is called Boundless. Because of its concealment from all creatures above and below, it is also called Nothingness. If one asks, "What is it?" the answer is, "Nothing," meaning: No one can understand anything about it. It is negated of every conception. No one can know anything about it—except the belief that it exists. Its existence cannot be grasped by anyone other than it. Therefore its name is "I am becoming."[96]

The universal Italian greeting *ciao* derives from *schiào,* (pronounced "skia-oh"). In the Venetian dialect, it means "slave," or "your servant." People start out humble and see how they get on.[97]

And on that note, Ciao!

---

[95] Coleman Barks and John Moyne, eds., *Rumi: Selected Poems* (New York: Penguin, 1995), p. 279.

[96] Daniel C. Matt, *The Essential Kabbalah: The Heart of Jewish Mysticism* (New York: HarperCollins, 1994), pp. 66–67.

[97] Beppe Severgnini, *La Bella Figura,* p. 181–182.

Acknowledgments

Thank you to all my teachers and brothers. A great thanks to Shayar Sr. and Shayar Jr. and to William Jens Jensen, Chris Bamford, Michael Lipson, Gene Gollogly, Georg Kühlwind, Orland Bishop, Dennis Klocek, Roger Gosselin, Fred Donohue, Leschek Forchek, Walter Goldstein, Walter M., and many others.

MARIE-LAURE VALANDRO was born in 1948 and spent her childhood in Bourgogne, Morocco, Algeria, and Bretagne. At fifteen, she moved with her family to Boston, where she received a B.A. in modern literature, romance languages, and education and taught in the Boston public school system. Later, she moved to Vermont, and obtained an M.A. in literature. At twenty-three, Marie-Laure returned to Paris to study at The Sorbonne, to teach and to travel around Europe to various Christian Holy sites. She later moved to Tehran to teach technical English and to tour throughout the Eastern world, studying Sufism, Zoroastrianism, Islam, Buddhism, and Hinduism as seen through the eyes of its believers and through visits to holy sites. Marie-Laure returned to the United States to care for her son. She lived in the community of Wilton, New Hampshire, where she first encountered Anthroposophy. She ended her school teaching to care for her daughter, son, and husband, a medical doctor. Meanwhile, she continued to travel and trek in South America, both alone and with her children. Later, she moved to Wisconsin and began the Liane Collot d'Herbois training in painting. On her family farm in Wisconsin, Marie-Laure uses biodynamic methods and has developed master gardens, vegetable gardens, herb gardens, and an orchard. She has also established a painting studio, where she creates large veil paintings. Recently, she moved from Wisconsin to a post-and-beam house built by her son in the Canadian Rockies of British Columbia. Her goal is to continue walking across this beautiful Earth, meeting people with love and sharing her journeys in meditative books, sprinkled with insights from Rudolf Steiner's works and the many talented students of his teachings. She continues to make large veil paintings to "heal people and spaces."

www.ingramcontent.com/pod-product-compliance
Lightning Source LLC
Chambersburg PA
CBHW031146160426

43193CB00008B/276